Responsible Money

RESPONSIBLE MONEY

A STANDARDS-BASED FINANCIAL CURRICULUM

teacher's manual

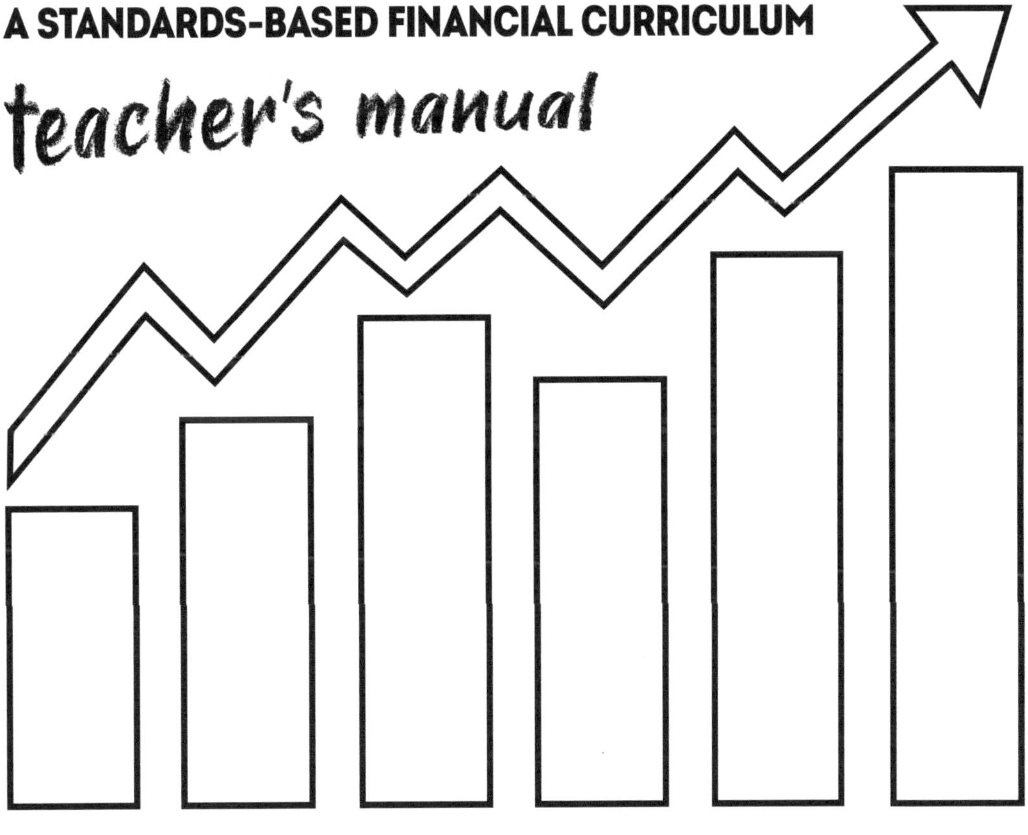

RON WRIGHT

The content of *Responsible Money* is for information purposes only. The reader should not construe any information as legal, tax, investment, financial, or other advice. All content is of a general nature and does not address the circumstances of any particular individual or entity. Nothing contained in *Responsible Money* constitutes a solicitation, recommendation, endorsement, or offer by the author Ron Wright, members of Bear Wright LLC, or any third party to buy or sell any securities or financial instruments. For specific legal, tax, investment, financial, or other advice, seek the assistance of a licensed professional.

PO Box 82 Flossmoor, IL 60422

Website: www.bearwrightllc.com

ISBN: 978-1-7379783-0-5

Library of Congress Control Number: 2022906214

Printed in the United States of America

First Printing, 2022

CONTENTS

FOREWORD

Financial literacy is one of the most important and impactful areas of study, but it is often disregarded in schools and community organizations. While studying the Responsible Money curriculum, students will be taught not just foundational skills, but how to acquire and hold on to wealth, so their money works for them. This can lead to positive outcomes and have a multigenerational impact. The curriculum is organized into six sessions that can coincide with a school quarter or be held as a small group course. These sessions include:

1. What Money Means to You
2. Sources of Money
3. Budgeting and Saving
4. Personal Banking
5. Understanding Credit
6. Responsible Investing

This curriculum can stand alone or be accompanied by mentor texts. The information is comprehensive and requires no prior financial knowledge or additional planning by teachers to deliver the instruction. *Responsible Money* is standards-based and aligned with Common Core, Council for Economic Education (CEE)®, Jump$tart®, Family and Consumer Sciences, and the C3 Framework for Social Studies.

Responsible Money was designed to help you explore your personal beliefs about money, dispel financial myths, and provide tips that can help you increase your financial stability. This program will also help you develop a budget; and budgeting is the first step toward financial freedom. Whether you are unemployed or making six figures, having a budget will help you to understand where your money is going. Budgeting will help you to identify and reduce overspending. Reducing your expenses increases your revenue, allowing you to save. Many Americans live paycheck to paycheck, regardless of their income. *Responsible Money* can lead you down the road to financial freedom.

Ron Wright is a graduate of Purdue University in West Lafayette, Indiana, with a bachelor's degree in electrical engineering. After working in the engineering and manufacturing fields for several years, he obtained his life & health insurance license, and later added the series 6, 63, and 65 licenses. He has worked in finance as a financial advisor and licensed banker. After working in the field, he later obtained a Master of Arts in education from Governors State University and an Illinois state-accredited teaching certificate. He has taught elementary and junior high school math for over ten years. The test scores of his students continuously exceed expectations for two reasons: He fosters the social and emotional development of his students and he helps them strive toward academic excellence. His teaching is not limited just to the state standards, but goes beyond them. Mr. Wright currently resides in Illinois with his wife and two sons.

Past Responsible Money program participants have said:

- "I can start saving now!"
- "I could have discussed this subject for three hours."
- "I feel that I will be successful at saving money. For the first time ever, I have a feeling that I can succeed."
- "This is a very helpful and important class to me because I really need to learn to budget my money."
- "Even at my age, I learned how to view money management differently."

I believe that the Responsible Money program is a necessary addition to our school curricula.

Lynette Campbell, MA EdS
School Administrator
School Psychologist

ACKNOWLEDGMENTS

I must first thank my mother, Delores Wright, who taught me my earliest lessons about banking. I still remember her taking me into the bank where she worked, when I was a kid with my savings passbook. Although she passed away in 2012, Mom taught me the importance of saving and giving.

Thank you to my father, Ron Wright, Sr. Your example taught me early lessons about real estate and investing in stocks.

Thank you to my wife, Tamira, for always challenging me to become a better person and for being the foundation of our family. Your love and support truly made this possible.

Thank you to my sons, Jeffrey and Matthew Wright. I love you more than you can imagine. You both are the reason why this curriculum exists. My strong desire to teach arose because I wanted you both to be prepared for your futures.

Thank you to my grandmother, Inez Traylor. Your life lessons have provided me with a strong foundation and have served me well.

Thank you, Dr. Peter K.B. St. Jean, for giving me the opportunity to create the Responsible Money curriculum for a large nonprofit in Chicago. Our work together not only helped the people we served, but it also helped me to become a better teacher and writer.

Thank you to my students, past and present. You truly inspire me to be my best and to remain a lifelong learner.

Thank you to my former colleagues. These financial professionals taught me countless lessons that I will never forget.

Thank you to my current school district, administration, and staff. The support you have given me during this process has been incredible.

And thank you to all my family and friends. Your love and support have helped beyond measure.

Responsible Money

Session 1
What Money Means to You

Description of Session:

This first session is designed to help participants explore their personal beliefs about money. The participants will consider why money is important in their lives and discover how they feel about past financial decisions. The participants will learn several important financial terms that we will use throughout this program.

Courtesy of Sharon McCutcheon via *Unsplash*.

Before the Session:

1. Gather needed materials including the following: *Responsible Money* workbooks for each participant, name tags, pens or pencils, flip chart, markers, and paper.

2. Make copies of pre-test handout for all participants.

3. Write the name(s) of the facilitator(s) on the flip chart.

4. Hang up posters and visual aids.

ACTIVITY 1.1 WELCOME AND PRE-TEST

Time: 25 minutes

Materials: *Responsible Money* workbooks, name tags, flip chart, markers, pens or pencils, pre-test handouts

Objective:

As a result of this activity, the participants will become more familiar with their fellow participants and begin forming a close, supportive group. Participants will receive the course materials and complete the pre-test.

Procedures:

The facilitator(s) will:

1. Greet participants with a handshake and an introduction as they enter the room.

2. Ask each participant to sign in and fill out a name tag.

3. Conduct an icebreaker activity and ask each participant to introduce themselves.

4. Explain the general format of the program as follows:

    - This six-week program consists of one two-hour session per week.
    - A ten-minute break will be given after the first hour.
    - Each session will begin at _____ and end at ____ (state each time).
    - Hand out copies of the *Responsible Money* workbook and explain that the workbook must be brought to each session.
    - We will begin with a pre-test. Then a post-test will be given at the end of the program.
    - Participants will complete a log at the end of each session. Using the log, they will record what they have learned and how it will help them in the future.
    - Money is an extremely personal matter and participants are asked not to share others' personal financial information with people outside the group.

5. As an important disclaimer, say: "The financial information provided in this course is general in nature and should not be considered as financial or tax advice. The facilitator of this program is not a licensed financial professional. For detailed financial advice, please seek a licensed financial professional."

ACTIVITY 1.2 WHAT MONEY MEANS TO YOU

Time: 30 minutes

Materials: *Responsible Money* workbooks, name tags, flip chart, markers, pens or pencils

Objective:

As a result of this activity, the participants will better understand and identify their beliefs about money. Participants will also begin to explore and understand how to better manage their personal finances.

Learning Competencies:

As a result of this activity, the participants will be able to:

1. Identify what is important to them about money.
2. Identify ways to make better use of their money.
3. Define various financial terms.

Procedures:

1. Ask participants to complete questions 1–4 on **page 3** in the workbook. These questions are as follows:
   - *Why is money important to you?*
   - *Why is the answer you provided for question 1 important to you?*
   - *Why is the answer you provided for question 2 important to you?*
   - *Why is the answer you provided for question 3 important to you?*
2. The facilitator(s) will give an example set of answers (e.g., "Money allows me to pay my bills. Paying bills is important because I need a place to live. Having a place to live is important because I can keep my family safe. Keeping my family safe is important because it makes me feel like a good provider.").
3. Ask for several volunteers to share their answers with the group.

4. If a participant is having trouble, restate the question in a different way (e.g., What is important about _________?).

5. This should be repeated until the answers have little to do with the money. The final answers should reveal the participants' core values and feelings (e.g., "Being a good provider will help me feel like a good father.").

(Break Time)

ACTIVITY 1.3 WAYS WE USE OUR MONEY

Time: 30 minutes

Materials: *Responsible Money* workbooks, calculators, name tags, flip chart, markers, pens or pencils

Objective:

To explore past financial decisions in order to determine their best and worst financial choices and to introduce the importance of saving.

Learning Competencies:

As a result of this activity, the participants will be able to:

1. Analyze their past financial decisions.
2. Identify recent purchases.
3. Identify unnecessary spending.

Procedures:

1. Ask participants to complete **questions 1 and 2** on **page 4** of the workbook ("the best thing I have done with money" and "the worst thing I have done with money").
2. Ask for volunteers to discuss their answers.
3. Ask participants to complete **questions 3–5** on **page 4** of the workbook.
4. Create two columns on the flip chart. Label one column "Most" and the other "Least," in terms of importance.
5. Discuss needs vs. wants.
6. Now ask the group to identify the cost of each item in the "Least" column.
7. Add up the total for the group.

8. Write the amount on the flip chart and say: "This is how much we could have saved as a group by choosing not to make our least important purchases."

Courtesy of Sharon McCutcheon via *Unsplash*.

9. Tell the group that we must begin saving small amounts of money because over time it adds up.

10. Ask the group if they have enough money to save. Wait for them to respond, noting that most will say "no."

11. Tell the group about the "Latte Factor®," a financial term that states how saving $5 per day (what we spend on our morning latte) for 5 years yields a savings of $9,125 without earning any interest. If you earned just 1.25% interest, you would have saved $9,405.98!

ACTIVITY 1.4 FINANCIAL TERMS

Time: 20 minutes

Materials: *Responsible Money* workbooks, name tags, flip chart, markers, pens or pencils

Objective:

To define several financial terms that will be used throughout the Responsible Money program.

Learning Competencies:

As a result of this activity, the participant will be able to:

1. Define various financial terms.
2. Understand the relationship between the terms.
3. Explain how these terms are used in their lives.

Procedures:

1. Tell the participants that the following terms will be defined: **bank, budget, expenses, finance, money**, and **revenue**.
2. Read the first term and then ask for a volunteer to read each additional term. Discuss each term after it is read. Avoid simply reading the terms and rushing through this activity. The definitions can be found on **page 5** of the *Responsible Money* workbook, as follows:
   - **Bank.** *A financial institution licensed to receive deposits. There are two types of banks: commercial/retail banks and investment banks. In most countries, banks are regulated by national government or central bank.*
   - **Budget.** *A budget is a spending plan which gives you a sense of how much money you can spend and how much you can save. A budget can be made for a person, family, group of people, business, government, country, multinational organization, or just about anything else that involves spending money. A budget shows the trade-off made when one good is exchanged for another.*

- **Expenses.** *Whatever you spend money on is an expense. Expenses are the financial costs a person or business incurs to fulfill their needs. In order to maximize profits, expenses must be kept to a minimum.*
- **Finance.** *This is the study of the creation and management of money. It involves banking, credit, investments, assets, and liabilities. Finance consists of financial systems, which include the public, private, and government sectors. Finance is sometimes divided into three categories: public, corporate, and personal.*
- **Money.** *An officially issued legal tender that is usually a paper currency and coin. Money is often synonymous with cash and other negotiable instruments such as checks. Each country has an official money or currency that is used as a medium of exchange within that country. Some countries, in areas such as the European Union and the Eastern Caribbean, share a common currency. One country's currency can usually be exchanged for another's at some banks and currency exchanges.*
- **Revenue.** *The amount of money a person or company receives during a specific period. Revenue is sometimes referred to as income or profit. In order to make the most profit, it is important to reduce expenses.*

3. Make sure you point out the relationship between expenses and revenue. It is important for the participants to learn to decrease expenses and to limit unneeded spending.

4. Ask the participants if they have any further questions or comments.

Notes

ACTIVITY 1.5 CLOSURE AND REFLECTION

Time: 15 minutes

Materials: *Responsible Money* workbooks, name tags, flip chart, markers, pens or pencils

Objective:

To assess what the group has learned and to reflect.

Learning Competencies:

As a result of this activity, the participants will be able to reflect on and think about their personal finances.

Procedures:

1. Ask the participants to answer the following two questions.

   - The Latte Factor® is a term that refers to:
     a. The importance of saving small amounts of money over time.
     b. Cutting out unneeded routine purchases and saving that money.
     c. A boycott on buying coffee.
     d. I'm not sure.
     e. Both a & b.

   Correct Answer: e

   - Revenue and expenses are related because:
     a. As revenue increases, expenses also increase.
     b. As expenses decrease, revenue increases.
     c. As expenses decrease, revenue decreases.
     d. There is no relation between revenue and expenses.
     e. I'm not sure.

   Correct Answer: b

2. Tell the participants to complete the following "What I Learned" Log, found on **page 6** of the *Responsible Money* workbook.

(Break Time)

"WHAT I LEARNED" LOG

One thing I learned today is:

____

____

____

____

____

Courtesy of Sharon McCutcheon via *Unsplash*.

On a scale of 0–5, how likely are you to use what you have learned in this session?

0 = Not at all likely 5 = Very likely

0 1 2 3 4 5

What I learned in this session will help me because:

____

____

____

____

____

____

____

____

Session 2
Sources of Money

Description of Session:

This session will focus on different sources of money. We will discuss our feelings about earning an income. We will also discuss the potential problems involved with getting money too quickly.

Courtesy of Avinash Kumar via *Unsplash*.

Before the Session:

1. Gather needed materials, including *Responsible Money* workbooks for each participant, name tags, pens or pencils, flip chart, markers, and paper.
2. Write the name(s) of the facilitator(s) on the flip chart.
3. Hang up posters and visual aids.

ACTIVITY 2.1 WARM-UP

Time: 20 minutes

Materials: *Responsible Money* workbooks, name tags, flip chart, markers, pens or pencils

Objective:

As a result of this session, the participants will be able to express their feelings about earning money, establish their career goals, and explore the pros and cons of earning money in various ways.

Procedures:

The facilitator(s) will:

1. Greet the participants with a handshake and an introduction as they enter the room.
2. Ask each participant to sign in and fill out a name tag.
3. As an important disclaimer, say: "The following information is general in nature and should not be considered as specific financial or tax advice. The facilitator of this program is not a licensed financial professional. For specific financial advice, please seek a licensed financial professional."
4. Read the following quote: "The darkest hour in any man's life is when he sits down to plan how to get money without earning it." —Horace Greeley
5. Ask the participants what this quote means to them personally. (Background information: Horace Greeley ran for President of the United States in 1872 and lost to Ulysses S. Grant. He was a newspaper editor and politician who strongly opposed slavery.)

The participants will:

1. Complete warm-up exercises 1–3 on **page 11** of the workbook. These exercises are as follows:
   - *To me, earning money means:* ______________________.
   - *The best part about earning money is:* ______________________.
   - *My career goal is:* ______________________.

2. Discuss their responses.

Notes

ACTIVITY 2.2 PITFALLS OF FAST MONEY

Time: 30 minutes

Materials: *Responsible Money* workbooks, name tags, flip chart, markers, pens or pencils

Objective:

As a result of this session, the participant will be able to identify many of the pitfalls of receiving a large lump sum of money without understanding how to use it properly.

Learning Competencies:

As a result of this activity, the participants will be able to:

1. Identify various ways they might respond to receiving a lump sum.
2. Identify why many lottery winners go broke.

Procedures:

1. Ask the participants to complete **page 12** of the workbook.

   Please rate yourself on a scale of 1–5 (1 being least likely, 5 being most likely) in the following scenario. Rank the following in order of most likely to least likely. Do not reuse a number.

   - *If I won the lottery, the first thing I would do is:* *(Suggested)*
   - *Make a major purchase (e.g., car, home).* ______ *(2)*
   - *Contact a financial professional and an attorney.* ______ *(5)*
   - *Give close family members money they need.* *gift tax ______ *(1)*
   - *Put the money in a bank.* ______ *(4)*
   - *Pay off all my bills.* ______ *(3)*

2. The facilitator will project the article, "19 Lottery Winners Who Blew It All," on available technology from: www.businessinsider. com/17-lottery-winners-who-blew-it-all-2013-5.

3. Read each scenario and briefly discuss each.

4. The facilitator(s) will state that no matter how much money you have, planning is essential.

Notes

ACTIVITY 2.3 PROS AND CONS

Time: 30 minutes

Materials: *Responsible Money* workbooks, name tags, flip chart, markers, pens or pencils

Objective:

As a result of this session, the participants will be able to analyze the pros and cons of various jobs.

Learning Competencies:

As a result of this session, the participant will be able to:

1. Identify the pros and cons of various types of employment.
2. Create their own scenario and identify its pros and cons.

Procedures:

The facilitator(s) will:

1. Read the following from **page 13** of the *Responsible Money* workbook.

   You can earn money in various ways. Whether you work in a factory, flip burgers, or practice medicine, all honest work has value and helps our society. List the pros and cons of earning money in the scenarios below.

2. Ask the participants to complete **pages 13–14** of the *Responsible Money* workbook.
3. Ask for volunteers to share the first scenario's pros and cons.
4. Use the flip chart to write out the pros and cons.
5. Read the pros and cons list created for the scenario.
6. Repeat steps 3–5 for the second scenario.

7. Ask participants to create their own scenario and identify its pros and cons.

8. Ask three volunteers to share the scenarios they created.

Notes

ACTIVITY 2.4 FINDING EMPLOYMENT

Time: 25 minutes

Materials: *Responsible Money* workbooks, name tags, flip chart, markers, pens or pencils

Objective:
To offer tips on finding employment.

Learning Competencies:
As a result of this session, the participant will:

1. Improve their job search.
2. Understand the importance of networking, volunteering, and job training.

Procedures:
The facilitator(s) will:

1. State that the following tips are not meant to replace a certified job training program.
2. Encourage enrollment in local training or job readiness courses.
3. Provide information on local job programs.

The participants will:

1. Volunteer to read the tips found on **page 15** of the workbook out loud.
2. Discuss each tip after it is read.

Page 15 of the workbook appears as follows:

> *If you are currently unemployed or underemployed, here are some tips that may help you with your job search.*
>
> - **Networking.** *Today people can stay connected better than any other time in human history. It is important to use social media to enhance your job search. Stay connected with people you know who work at various*

organizations. Have a friend or associate who is in good standing with their employer put in a good word for you.

- **Job Training.** *Find a local job training program. Most employers today want employees who can make an immediate impact. In other words, they want people who can hit the ground running. The more skills you have, the more marketable you will be.*
- **Education.** *Whatever your level of education you currently possess, seek to increase it. In today's job market, we must be lifetime learners. As technology changes it becomes more important to stay current. An investment in your own education shows future employers that you are goal-oriented and self-motivated.*
- **Being Honest.** *The days of padding the resume are over. It is far too easy for employers to obtain reliable employee background information. Furthermore, being honest and open with future employers ensures that you find the job that truly matches your skills, interests, and abilities.*
- **Updating Your Resume.** *Keep your resume current. Look up various job descriptions and use similar language found in the descriptions on your resume. Companies often use computer programs to scan resumes to look for key words and phrases. Using the correct language on your resume can make a huge difference.*
- **Volunteering.** *Make it a priority to volunteer in your community. This may provide you with references and could even lead to employment with the organization where you volunteer. Volunteering will help you meet people and meeting people can lead to employment. And finally, volunteering gives you purpose and the ability to improve important work-related skills.*

Notes

ACTIVITY 2.5 CLOSURE AND REFLECTION

Time: 15 minutes

Materials: *Responsible Money* workbooks, name tags, markers, pens or pencils

Objective:
To assess what the group has learned and to reflect.

Learning Competencies:
As a result of this activity, the participants will be able to reflect and think about various sources of income.

Procedures:

1. Ask the participants to answer the following two questions.
   - Volunteer work has several benefits, including:
     a. A chance to get references.
     b. Work experience.
     c. Networking opportunities.
     d. Potential employment.
     e. All of the above.

   Correct Answer: e

   - Resumes today are:
     a. Often pre-screened by computers for key words and phrases.
     b. Thrown in the garbage immediately.
     c. Never pre-screened.
     d. Unnecessary.
     e. All of the above.

   Correct Answer: a

2. Tell the participants to complete the following “What I Learned” Log, found on **page 16** of the *Responsible Money* workbook.

"WHAT I LEARNED" LOG

Courtesy of Avinash Kumar via *Unsplash*.

One thing I learned today is:

On a scale of 0–5, how likely are you to use what you have learned in this session?

0 = Not at all likely 5 = Very likely

0 1 2 3 4 5

What I learned in this session will help me because:

Session 3
Budget and Saving

Description of Session:

Courtesy of Andre Taissin via *Unsplash*.

This session will provide participants with ways to begin budgeting and saving their money. Participants will gain tips on how to create a budget and how to plan their own personal budget. Participants will also learn ways to begin a savings plan. Finally, we will discuss savings rates in the United States and look for ways to overcome the challenge of saving money.

Before the Session:

1. Gather needed materials including the following: *Responsible Money* workbooks for each participant, calculators, name tags, pens or pencils, flip chart, markers, and paper.

2. Write the name(s) of the facilitator(s) on the flip chart.

3. Hang up posters and visual aids.

ACTIVITY 3.1 WARM-UP

Time: 10 minutes

Materials: *Responsible Money* workbooks, name tags, flip chart, markers, pens or pencils

Objective:

As a result of this session, the participants will be able to identify whether they have had a budget, identify their feelings about budgeting money, and identify ways they can begin to save money.

Procedures:

The facilitator(s) will:

1. Greet the participants with a handshake as they enter the room.
2. Ask each participant to sign in and fill out a name tag.
3. Say: "This session will allow you to create a personal budget. Please remember that money is a very personal matter, so please keep specific information confidential."
4. Read the following quote from the top of **page 21** in the *Responsible Money* workbook: "Many folks think they aren't good at earning money, when what they don't know is how to use it." —Frank A. Clark

The participants will:

1. Complete warm-up exercises 1–3 on **page 21** of the workbook. These exercises are as follows:

   The last time I was on a budget was: ____________________________
   I think that a budget is: ____________________________________
   One way I can improve my savings is: __________________________

2. Share their responses.
3. Discuss their responses and feelings about these statements.
4. Discuss ways they believe they can improve budgeting and saving.

Notes

ACTIVITY 3.2 BUDGETING TIPS

Time: 30 minutes

Materials: *Responsible Money* workbooks, name tags, flip chart, markers, pens or pencils

Objective:

To read and discuss the six steps to creating a successful budget.

Procedures:

The facilitator(s) will:

1. Read the following from **page 22** of the *Responsible Money* workbook.

   In Session 1, we defined a budget as a spending plan which gives you a sense of how much money you can spend and how much you can save. To create an effective budget, we can follow six steps.

2. Ask for volunteers to read the six budgeting steps found on **page 22** of the workbook. These steps are:

   - **Know What You Make.** *This may seem simple, but many people do not read their pay stubs from work. Paychecks can sometimes be incorrect. Knowing what you are supposed to make may help you find lost money.*
   - **Know What You Spend.** *Again, this may sound simple, but most people have no idea where each and every dollar goes each month. No matter what your income is, knowledge is power. Knowing where your money goes each month is essential to finding areas where you can save money.*
   - **Set Realistic Spending Limits.** *If you go to the movies every weekend, put that into your budget. Some expenses, like food, never go away. If your budget only allows $20 for food, it needs to be adjusted.*
   - **Keep It Simple.** *When creating a budget, begin by keeping receipts for all transactions. At the end of each day, add up what you have spent and record totals in the appropriate categories on a budget worksheet. Keep a rolling total for at least one month. By the end of the*

month, you will know how much you spent on things like entertainment, food, clothes, etc. This will give you a more accurate idea of your spending habits and help you create realistic spending limits. You can also do this with various computer programs, but the key is to keep it simple. One helpful website you can try is www.budgetworksheets.org.

- **Accountability.** *Trying to go it alone usually doesn't work. Few people have the discipline needed to stick with a budget by themselves. In order to be successful at maintaining a budget, find a reliable person to help you stay on track. Whether it's a parent, spouse, friend, or a trusted financial professional, accountability is a key component to successful budgeting.*
- **Don't Stop.** *To reach your savings goal, budgeting should become a way of life. The longer you commit to budgeting, the easier it becomes. Always look for ways to reduce spending, like clipping coupons and shopping for bargains. Budgeting helps you identify your spending habits, which will help you reduce unnecessary expenses. So get going and keep it up!*

3. Make sure the group discusses each step before moving on to the next.

4. Ask if anyone has questions or additional comments.

Notes

ACTIVITY 3.3 CREATING A BUDGET

Time: 30 minutes

Materials: *Responsible Money* workbooks, calculators, name tags, flip chart, markers, pens or pencils

Objective:
To create a budget plan.

Learning Competencies:
As a result of this activity, the participants will create a personal budget, identify their spending habits, and find areas where they overspend.

Procedures:
The facilitator(s) will:

1. Say: "Now it is time for you to create a budget plan."
2. Tell participants: "Failing to plan is planning to fail, so let's begin."
3. Tell participants to complete the budget worksheet found on **pages 23 and 24** of the *Responsible Money* workbook.
4. Mention that these categories may not all apply to you and your life. An example of this may be childcare expenses. If your children are adults or you are not a parent, then you would not list any expense in that column. The following tables are in the *Responsible Money* workbook.

Deductions	Budget	Actual	Difference
Savings	$	$	$
Child Support	$	$	$
Alimony	$	$	$
Other	$	$	$

Housing	Budget	Actual	Difference
Rent or Mortgage	$	$	$
Utilities	$	$	$
Insurance	$	$	$
Other	$	$	$

Food	Budget	Actual	Difference
Groceries	$	$	$
Dining Out	$	$	$
Coffee	$	$	$
Other	$	$	$

Transportation	Budget	Actual	Difference
Car Payment	$	$	$
Public Transport	$	$	$
Parking	$	$	$
Other	$	$	$

Debt Payments	Budget	Actual	Difference
Credit Cards	$	$	$
Student Loans	$	$	$
Other Loans	$	$	$
Other	$	$	$

Family	Budget	Actual	Difference
Childcare	$	$	$
Activities	$	$	$
Pet Care	$	$	$
Other	$	$	$

Personal	Budget	Actual	Difference
Clothing	$	$	$
Hair Care	$	$	$
Toiletries	$	$	$
Other	$	$	$

Miscellaneous	Budget	Actual	Difference
Charity	$	$	$
Entertainment	$	$	$
Education	$	$	$
Other	$	$	$

Summary	Budget	Actual	Difference
Total Expenses	$	$	$

5. Tell the group: "Now it's time to total your numbers."

Have the participants evaluate their budgets. Mention that the total budget should equal their monthly income and that the actual amount should equal the budgeted amount. Any surplus is to be redirected to the savings column.

ACTIVITY 3.4 SAVING MONEY

Time: 30 minutes

Materials: *Responsible Money* workbooks, name tags, flip chart, markers, pens or pencils

Objective:
To provide participants with tips to help increase their savings.

Learning Competencies:
As a result of this activity, participants will learn five tips to help increase their savings.

Procedures:
The facilitator(s) will:

1. Say: "This session is meant to help you start saving today."

2. Read the following paragraph from **page 25** of the *Responsible Money* workbook:

   As you can see, budgeting is truly the first step to a successful savings plan. Most people believe saving is important. However, many people find it challenging to save money. People often say they can't afford to save money. The truth is that you can't afford not to save. The less money you earn, the more important it is to save. Here are some tips to help you begin saving today.

3. Ask for volunteers to read the following five savings tips from **page 25** of the workbook.

   - **Pay Yourself First.** *Notice that the first entry into the budget worksheet above was for your savings amount. Saving must be number one on the list. In order for your savings plan to work, it must become part of your regular routine. Don't wait—start saving today.*
   - **Start Small.** *Remember the Latte Factor® we discussed in Session 1? The fact is: saving $5 per day for one year amounts to $1,825. Saving $5 each day for five years equals a savings of $9,125, without earning any interest.*

If you earned just 1.25% interest, you would save $9,405.98!

- **Make It Automatic.** *Technology today has made it easier to save. Unfortunately, with 24-hour access to our money, it is also easier to spend. That's why saving must be automatic. Many employers offer direct deposit and will split your pay between multiple accounts. Have a portion of each paycheck go automatically to your savings account. If this is not an option for you, your bank can set up automatic transfers between your checking and savings accounts. These transfers can be set up online through your bank's website or by visiting your bank in person.*
- **Set a Goal.** *Create savings goals that are both short-term and long-term. Goals vary from person to person. For example, you may want to have $500 in the bank by the end of the year.*
- **Don't Stop.** *Just like budgeting, saving must become a routine. Look for ways to increase your savings. If you must temporarily decrease your routine savings amount because of the budget, that's fine; but don't stop saving.*

The participants will:

1. Discuss why each step is important.
2. Discuss any challenges they face in following each step.
3. Discuss ways to overcome any challenges.

Notes

ACTIVITY 3.5 US SAVINGS STATISTICS (OPTIONAL ACTIVITY)

Time: 10 minutes

Materials: *Responsible Money* workbooks, name tags, flip chart, markers, pens or pencils

Objective:

To share US statistical data regarding savings in the United States.

Learning Competencies:

As a result of this activity, the participants will better understand that saving is a challenge for all Americans and that they should not feel alone.

Procedures:

The facilitator(s) will:

1. Ask participants to review the graphs found on **page 26** of the *Responsible Money* workbook.
2. Explain that the first graph shows the US household savings rates as a percentage of disposable income.
3. Define disposable income as the amount of money available after taxes are withheld.
4. Explain that the second graph shows the US personal savings rate compared to personal credit card debt.
5. State that the data shows Americans are saving less than half of what they saved fifty years ago. Even as the amount of credit card debt decreases, savings have continued to decrease in the years since the 2008 financial crisis. The data used was available through the end of 2012.

Personal Saving vs. Credit Card Debt
(% of Disposable Income)

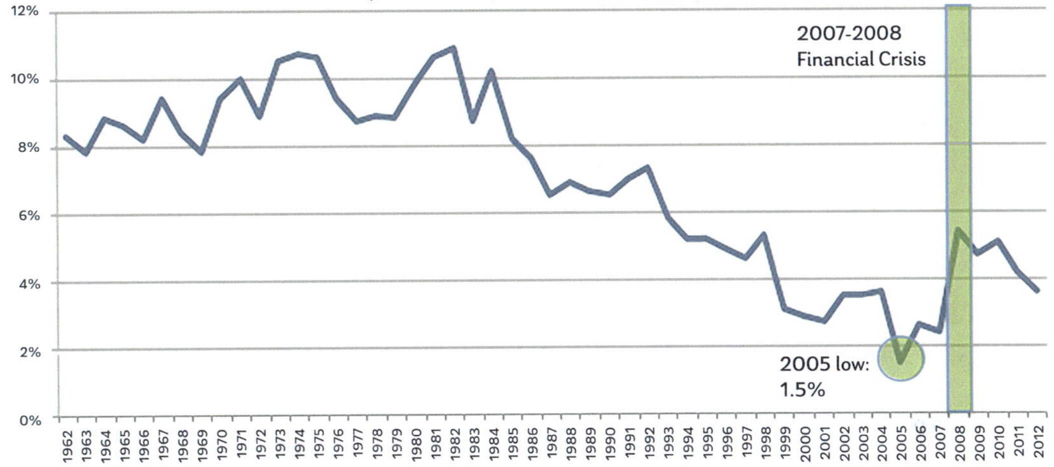

Personal Saving
(% of Disposable Income)

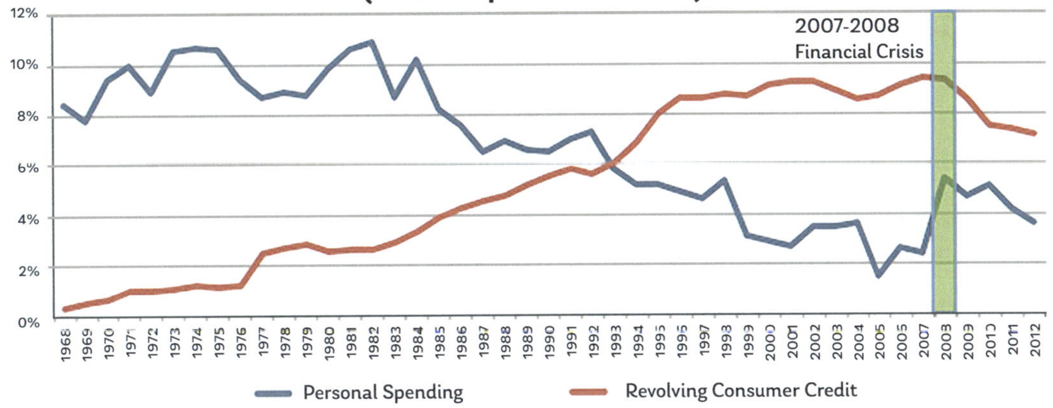

The graphs are from page 26 of the workbook.
Source: "American Personal Savings Rate Statistics through 2012," NerdWallet®
(www.nerdwallet.com/blog/banking/american-personal-saving-rate).

Notes

ACTIVITY 3.6 CLOSURE AND REFLECTION

Time: 10 minutes

Materials: *Responsible Money* workbooks, name tags, flip chart, markers, pens or pencils

Objective:
To assess what the group has learned and to reflect.

Learning Competencies:
As a result of this activity, the participants will be able to reflect and think about how they can begin budgeting and saving.

Procedures:
1. Participants will answer the following questions.

   - Today, Americans are saving:
     a. More than half of what they saved fifty years ago.
     b. Less than half of what they saved fifty years ago.
     c. The same amount they saved fifty years ago.
     d. Too little to worry about.
     e. None of the above.

   Correct Answer: b

   - The six steps to budgeting include all except:
     a. Accountability.
     b. Keeping it simple.
     c. Making more money.
     d. Knowing what you earn.
     e. Knowing what you spend.

   Correct Answer: c

2. Tell the participants to complete the following "What I Learned" Log, found on **page 27** of the *Responsible Money* workbook.

"WHAT I LEARNED" LOG

Courtesy of Andre Taissin via *Unsplash*.

One thing I learned today is:

On a scale of 0–5, how likely are you to use what you have learned in this session?

0 = Not at all likely 5 = Very likely

0 1 2 3 4 5

What I learned in this session will help me because:

Notes

Session 4
Personal Banking

Courtesy of Campaign Creators via *Unsplash*.

Description of Session:

This session will focus on understanding banking terms and account types, as well as avoiding common banking mistakes.

Before the Session:

1. Gather needed materials including the following: *Responsible Money* workbooks for each participant, calculators, name tags, pens or pencils, flip chart, markers, and paper.

2. Write the name(s) of the facilitator(s) on the flip chart.

3. Hang up posters and visual aids.

ACTIVITY 4.1 WARM-UP

Time: 10 minutes

Materials: *Responsible Money* workbooks, name tags, flip chart, markers, pens or pencils

Objective:
To discuss past banking issues and to encourage participants to establish a banking relationship.

Learning Competencies:
As a result of this session, the participants will be able to identify how they feel about banking and share past banking experiences.

Procedures:
The facilitator(s) will:

1. Greet the participants with a handshake as they enter the room.
2. Ask each participant to sign in and fill out a name tag.

The participants will:

1. Complete warm-up exercises 1–3 on **page 33** of the workbook. These exercises are as follows:

    a. *When I think of banking, I feel:* ____________________
    ____
    ____
    ____

    a. *Describe a positive past banking experience.* __________
    ____
    ____
    ____

    b. *Describe a negative past banking experience.* __________
    ____
    ____
    ____

2. Discuss their feelings regarding past banking experiences.

Note to Facilitator(s): This discussion should be brief. Do not allow it to get too negative. But be prepared because many people have had difficult relationships with banks.

ACTIVITY 4.2 BANKING SCENARIOS

Time: 20 minutes

Materials: *Responsible Money* workbooks, name tags, flip chart, markers, pens or pencils

Objective:

To discuss past banking issues and to encourage participants to understand their accounts.

Procedures:

1. Say: "This session will inform you about issues with banking in the twenty-first century."

2. Ask for two volunteers to perform the following banking scenarios:

Scenario 1: Positive Banking Experience

- **Teller:** "Welcome to XYZ Bank. How can I help you today?"
- **Customer:** "I would like to make a withdrawal from my checking account."
- **Teller:** "No problem, Mr. (or Mrs.) Doe."
- **Customer:** *Pretends to hand teller the withdrawal slip and their ID.*
- **Teller:** "Will that be all for today?"
- **Customer:** "Yep, that's it for today."
- **Teller:** *Pretends to hand customer the money and return the ID, while saying*, "Thank you and I look forward to seeing you soon."

Scenario 2: Negative Banking Experience

- **Teller:** "Welcome to XYZ Bank. How can I help you today?"
- **Customer:** "I would like to make a withdrawal from my checking account."
- **Teller:** "Just so you know, there will be a $5 convenience fee. Would you like to continue this transaction?"
- **Customer:** "I don't want to pay a fee to get my own money. May I speak to the manager?"

- **Teller:** "The manager is assisting another customer right now. Feel free to use our ATM in the lobby."
- **Customer, (yelling now):** "I only want $10 and, if you charge me a fee, that will cause me to bounce a check I wrote this morning."

3. Now ask the participants to discuss ways that Scenario 2 might have been avoided and write these responses on the flip chart.

ACTIVITY 4.3 BANKING TERMS

Time: 15 minutes

Materials: *Responsible Money* workbooks, calculators, name tags, flip chart, markers, pens or pencils

Objective:

To identify and define several banking terms.

Learning Competencies:

As a result of this activity, the participants will:

1. Be introduced to several banking terms.
2. Have a better understanding of banking.

Procedures:

1. Ask for volunteers to read the definitions found on **pages 35–37** of the *Responsible Money* workbook. The terms are as follows:

    - **Available Balance.** *The balance of an account less any hold, uncollected funds, and restrictions against the account.*
    - **Certificate of Deposit (CD).** *A negotiable instrument issued by a bank in exchange for funds, usually bearing interest, deposited with the bank.*
    - **Check 21 Act.** *Check 21 is a federal law designed to enable banks to handle more checks electronically, which is intended to make check processing faster and more efficient. Check 21 is the short name for the Check Clearing for the 21st Century Act, which went into effect on October 28, 2004.*
    - **ChexSystems.** *The ChexSystems, Inc. network is comprised of member financial institutions that regularly contribute information on mishandled checking and savings accounts to a central location. ChexSystems shares this information among member institutions to help them assess the risk of opening new accounts. ChexSystems only shares information with the member institutions;*

it does not decide on new account openings. Generally, information remains on ChexSystems for five years.

- **Debit Card.** *A debit card allows the account owner to access their funds electronically. Debit cards may be used to obtain cash from automated teller machines or to purchase goods or services using point-of-sale systems. The use of a debit card involves immediate debiting and crediting of consumers' accounts.*
- **Federal Deposit Insurance Corporation (FDIC).** *A government corporation that insures the deposits of all national and state banks that are members of the Federal Reserve System.*
- **Hold.** *Used to indicate that a certain amount of a customer's balance may not be withdrawn until an item has been collected or until a specific check or debit has posted.*
- **Insufficient Funds.** *When a depositor's checking account balance is inadequate to pay a check presented for payment.*
- **Interest.** *The term interest is used to describe the cost of using money.*
- **Kiting.** *Writing a check in an amount that will overdraw the account, but making up the deficiency by depositing another check from another bank. For example, mailing a check for the mortgage when your checking account has insufficient funds to cover the check, but counting on receiving and depositing your paycheck before the mortgage company presents the check for payment.*
- **Maturity.** *The date on which the principal balance of a loan, bond, or other financial instrument becomes due and payable.*
- **Minimum Balance.** *The amount of money required to be on deposit in an account to qualify the depositor for special services or to waive a service charge.*
- **Money Market Deposit Account.** *A savings account that offers a higher rate of interest in exchange for larger-than-normal deposits. Insured by the FDIC, these accounts have limits on the number of transactions allowed and may require higher balances to receive the higher rate of interest.*
- **Service Charge.** *A charge assessed by a depository institution for processing transactions and maintaining accounts.*

2. Share other definitions if participants ask or if they come up in context of the discussion. These may include the following:

   - **Account History.** The payment history of an account over a specific period of time, including the number of times the account was past due or over limit.
   - **Annual Percentage Rate (APR).** The cost of credit on a yearly basis, expressed as a percentage.
   - **Annual Percentage Yield (APY).** A percentage rate reflecting the total amount of interest paid on a deposit account based on the interest rate and the frequency of compounding for a 365-day year.
   - **Automated Clearing House (ACH).** A computerized facility used by member depository institutions to electronically combine, sort, and distribute inter-bank credits and debits. ACHs process electronic transfers of government securities and provides customer services, such as direct deposit of customers' salaries and government benefit payments (i.e., social security, welfare, and veterans' entitlements), as well as preauthorized transfers.
   - **Automatic Bill Payment.** A checkless system for paying recurring bills with one authorization statement to a financial institution. For example, the customer would only have to provide one authorization form/letter/document to pay the cable bill each month. The necessary debits and credits are made through an Automated Clearing House (ACH).
   - **Balance Transfer.** The process of moving an outstanding balance from one credit card to another. This is usually done to obtain a lower interest rate on the outstanding balance. Transfers are sometimes subjected to a balance transfer fee.
   - **Beneficiary.** A person who is entitled to receive the benefits or proceeds of a will, trust, insurance policy, retirement plan, annuity, or other contract.
   - **Bond, US Savings.** Savings bonds are issued in face value denominations by the US Government in denominations ranging from $50 to $10,000. They are typically long-term, low-risk investment tools.
   - **Cashier's Check.** A check drawn on the funds of the bank, not against the funds in a depositor's account. However, the depositor pays for the cashier's check with funds from their account. The primary benefit of a cashier's check is that the recipient of the check is assured that the funds are available.

- **Cut-off Time.** A time of day established by a bank for receipt of deposits. After the cut-off time, deposits are considered received on the next banking day.

Source: http://www.helpwithmybank.gov/dictionary/index-dictionary.html

Note to Facilitator(s): Direct participants to the glossary at the back of their workbooks if they would like to read and learn more banking terms. Focus the discussion on terms that may be unfamiliar like Check 21, ChexSystems, and kiting. Feel free to share all or some of the terms listed above if time permits.

Notes

ACTIVITY 4.4 COMMON BANKING CONCERNS

Time: 20 minutes

Materials: *Responsible Money* workbooks, calculators, name tags, flip chart, markers, pens or pencils

Objective:

To identify and discuss several common banking concerns.

Learning Competencies:

As a result of this activity, the participants will be able to:

1. Identify many common banking concerns.
2. Ask better questions when searching for a new bank.
3. Understand how to avoid some common banking problems.

Procedures:

1. Write the words "Past Problems" on the flip chart. Ask the participants to brainstorm any of their past banking problems and record them on the chart.
2. Tell the participants that many banking issues can be placed under two categories: availability of funds and fees.
3. Now draw a vertical line down the center of the next blank page of the flip chart, creating two columns. Label the columns "Available $" and "Fees."
4. Now try to place the concerns from the previous page into one of these categories. If the concern can't be placed under one of these, they may fall into categories like customer service, location, fraud, or other factors that are too specific for this discussion.
5. Read the following from **page 38** of the *Responsible Money* workbook.

   Availability of Funds: *There are several reasons why a bank may delay the availability of money in your account. Banks have different* *policies regarding funds availability. Your account agreement will outline your bank's funds availability policy. Here are some reasons for delays on the availability of funds, also known as extended holds.*

6. Ask for a volunteer to read each of the following reasons from **page 38**.

    - **Bad Checks.** *A check that was deposited into your account may have raised a "red flag." This means that you may have been given a bad check. If so, the hold placed on those funds will help prevent you from spending money that will never become available.*
    - **Redeposited Checks.** *Checks that have been returned once and are then redeposited will be placed on hold.*
    - **New Accounts.** *Typically, banks will hold funds longer when an account is less than thirty days old.*
    - **Account History.** *The better your banking history, the faster your funds will be available. For example, frequent overdrafts will lead to longer holds on your account.*
    - **Size Matters.** *Checks larger than $5,000 will be subjected to a hold. This includes payroll, government, and official checks. In these cases, the first $5,000 may be available, while any amount above $5,000 is held.*

7. Provide tips that will help the participants avoid these issues. These tips may include the following:

    - To avoid receiving bad checks, only accept checks from sources you trust. For example, if you have a feeling that a friend has given you a bad check, ask them if they will pay you back in cash.
    - Do not accept checks from people who have given you bad checks in the past. If a check you deposited is returned to you unpaid, don't try to redeposit the check. Inform the person who gave you the check that it was returned for insufficient funds and ask them for another form of payment.
    - Before you open any banking account, make sure you understand how it works. Most new accounts will have extended holds for the first thirty days. During this first thirty days, deposit cash when possible or sign up for direct deposit, if available. Funds that are deposited as cash or through direct deposit are available right away.
    - Remember to balance your checkbook daily. By keeping your account balanced at all times, you will be able to bring your ledger

and prove that charges on your account are incorrect, if a bank error occurs. Balancing your checkbook is the best way to catch any strange activity on your account and to maintain a positive account history.

- Only use apps and websites that you trust. Regular use of your bank's app is a great way to keep track of your account activity. However, it is your responsibility to know what you have spent. The bank only knows what items have been presented. Some other apps have reoccurring subscription fees that can add additional charges to your bank account.

ACTIVITY 4.5 BENEFITS OF BANKING

Time: 20 minutes

Materials: *Responsible Money* workbooks, calculators, name tags, flip chart, markers, pens or pencils

Objective:

To identify and discuss five benefits of banking.

Learning Competencies:

As a result of this activity, the participants will be able to identify five benefits of banking.

Procedures:

1. Ask the participants to find the "Benefits of Banking" list on **page 40** of the *Responsible Money* workbook.

2. Share the following five benefits:

   - **Safety.** *Keeping your money in a bank is much safer than putting it under your mattress or carrying it around. No matter where you live, keeping large amounts of cash is not a good idea. If your money is lost or stolen, you will not be able to get it back. If you found $300 on the ground, what would you do? Furthermore, US bank accounts are insured. The FDIC will replace your money up to $250,000, even if the bank fails.*
   - **Avoiding Check-Cashing Fees.** *If you receive a check of any kind, you must cash it. If you cash your check at a currency exchange, you will be charged a fee. Banks also charge check-cashing fees for non-customers. Although these fees may seem small, they add up over time (remember the Latte Factor®).*
   - **Ease of Paying Bills.** *Most people have bills. Having a checking account allows you to pay your bills by writing a check or paying them online. Without a checking account, you will have to pay fees for money orders or cashier's checks. Again, these fees add up over time. Online bill pay is free and it helps you pay bills quickly. With online bill pay, many bills receive the funds the next day. This can help you avoid late fees and avoiding fees is another way to increase your savings.*

- **Improves Your Chances of Getting Loans.** *Having a relationship with a bank can help you get loans in the future. Banks are more likely to lend money to their own customers. Even if your credit is less than perfect, having an established and positive banking relationship helps. Banking may also help you secure loans outside your bank. One of the first questions on a loan application is whether you have a checking or savings account with a positive balance.*
- **Earning Interest.** *Although interest rates on savings accounts and CDs are low, they are still higher than zero. Zero percent is the rate if you keep your money at home. Earning interest helps you make money and offset the rate of inflation. The more money you save, the more money you will earn in interest.*

3. Share other benefits like getting an ATM or debit card, which gives you greater access to the money in the account.

4. Allow participants to discuss these benefits.

Notes

ACTIVITY 4.6 CLOSURE AND REFLECTION

Time: 20 minutes

Materials: *Responsible Money* workbooks, calculators, name tags, flip chart, markers, pens or pencils

Objective:
To reflect, review, and assess the various aspects of personal banking discussed in this session.

Learning Competencies:
As a result of this activity, the participants will demonstrate their knowledge of personal banking.

Procedures:
The facilitator(s) will:

1. Ask participants to answer the following two questions.

   - The benefits of banking include all the following **except:**
     a. Earning interest.
     b. Guaranteed loan approval.
     c. Avoiding check-cashing fees.
     d. Safety.

   Correct Answer: b (Banking does not guarantee loan approval.)

   - A bank can place an extended hold on funds for all of the following **except:**
     a. Frequent overdrafts.
     b. Redeposited checks.
     c. Random account holds.
     d. New accounts.

   Correct Answer: c

2. Once they have completed the assessment, share the correct answers.

3. Tell the participants to complete the following "What I Learned" Log, found on **page 43** of the *Responsible Money* workbook.

"WHAT I LEARNED" LOG

Courtesy of Campaign Creators via *Unsplash*.

One thing I learned today is:

On a scale of 0–5, how likely are you to use what you have learned in this session?

0 = Not at all likely 5 = Very likely

0 1 2 3 4 5

What I learned in this session will help me because:

Notes

Session 5
Understanding Credit

Courtesy of rupixen.com via *Unsplash*.

Description of Session:

This session will focus on understanding how credit works. Participants will discuss common misconceptions about credit and learn tips for improving their credit score.

Before the Session:

1. Gather needed materials including the following: *Responsible Money* workbooks for each participant, calculators, name tags, pens or pencils, flip chart, markers, and paper.

2. Make copies of assessment handout for all participants.

3. Write the name(s) of the facilitator(s) on the flip chart.

4. Hang up posters and visual aids.

ACTIVITY 5.1 WARM-UP

Time: 10 minutes

Materials: *Responsible Money* workbooks, name tags, flip chart, markers, pens or pencils

Objective:

To gain a better understanding of how participants feel about credit.

Learning Competencies:

As a result of this session, the participants will be able to:

1. Identify their feelings about their past credit.
2. Identify common credit myths.
3. Improve their credit score.

Procedures:

The facilitator(s) will:

1. Greet the participants with a handshake as they enter the room.
2. Ask each participant to sign in and fill out a name tag.
3. Read the quote from the top of **page 49** of the *Responsible Money* workbook: "Creditors have better memories than debtors." —Benjamin Franklin

The participants will:

1. Complete warm-up exercises 1–3 on **page 49** of the workbook. These exercises are as follows:
    - *When I think of credit, I feel:* ______________________________
    - *I would describe my current credit status as:* __________________
    - *I could improve my credit score if I:* _________________________
2. Discuss the warm-up exercises.

3. Act out the following skit:

Scene 1

- **Character 1:** *Sitting down watching television, while the phone rings.*
- **Character 2:** *Walks in the room.* "Are you going to answer that?"
- **Character 1:** "I can't. It's a bill collector. Let it go to voicemail."

ACTIVITY 5.2 HOW CREDIT WORKS

Time: 20 minutes

Materials: *Responsible Money* workbooks, name tags, flip chart, markers, pens or pencils

Objective:

To provide a better understanding of how credit works.

Learning Competencies:

As a result of this session, the participants will be able to better explain how the US credit system works.

Procedures:

The facilitator(s) will:

1. Ask participants to look at Figure 5.1 on **page 51** of the *Responsible Money* workbook.

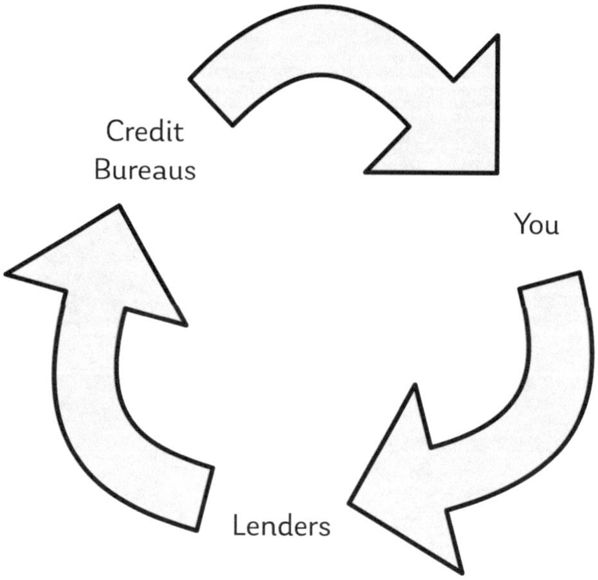

Figure 5.1: Credit Cycle

2. Explain that this cycle is often incomplete because people do not request their annual credit report.

3. Ask a participant to read the following from **page 51**:

   Figure 5.1 above illustrates the basic credit cycle. There are three main parts to our credit system. The first part is you, the American consumer. The next part is made up of the hundreds of lenders available to consumers. Lenders can range from large financial institutions to the local payday loan business. These lenders can then report your payment history to one or all of the three major credit bureaus. While there are other credit reporting bureaus, the three main ones are: TransUnion, Equifax, and Experian. These bureaus receive payment records every thirty days. On-time payments lead to good credit scores.

ACTIVITY 5.3 CREDIT TERMS (OPTIONAL ACTIVITY)

Time: 20 minutes

Materials: *Responsible Money* workbooks, name tags, flip chart, markers, pens or pencils

Objective:

To increase awareness and understanding of common terms used to describe credit.

Learning Competencies:

As a result of this session, the participants will be able to better identify common credit terms and their definitions.

Procedures:

The facilitator(s) will:

1. Read the definitions found on **page 52** of the *Responsible Money* workbook, as follows:

    - **Charge-off.** *The balance on a credit obligation that a lender no longer expects to be repaid and writes off as a bad debt.*
    - **Collection Agency.** *A company hired by a creditor to collect a debt that is owed. Creditors typically hire a collection agency only after they have made efforts to collect the debt themselves, usually through letters and telephone calls.*
    - **Credit Bureau.** *An agency that collects individual credit information and sells it for a fee to creditors so they can decide whether to grant a loan. Typical clients include banks, mortgage lenders, credit card companies, and other financing companies. Also commonly referred to as a consumer reporting agency or a credit reporting agency.*
    - **Credit Card.** *A card issued by a financial company giving the holder an option to borrow funds, usually at point of sale. Credit cards charge interest and are primarily used*

for short-term financing. Interest usually begins one month after a purchase is made and borrowing limits are pre-set according to the individual's credit rating.

- **Credit Report.** *A detailed report of an individual's credit history prepared by a credit bureau and used by a lender to determine a loan applicant's creditworthiness.*
- **Credit Score.** *A number, roughly between 300 and 850, that measures an individual's creditworthiness. The most well-known type of credit score is the FICO® score.*
- **Debit Card.** *A debit card allows the account owner to access their funds electronically. Debit cards may be used to obtain cash from automated teller machines or to purchase goods or services using point-of-sale systems. The use of a debit card involves immediate debiting and crediting of consumers' accounts.*
- **FICO® Score.** *A type of credit score that makes up a large portion of the credit report that lenders use to assess an applicant's credit risk and whether to extend a loan. FICO® is an acronym for the Fair Isaac Corporation, the creators of the FICO® score. The FICO® score is the most commonly used credit score.*

2. Allow time to discuss the terms, highlighting the difference between a debit card and a credit card.

3. Inform participants that more financial terms can be found in the glossary at the back of their workbooks.

Notes

____

____

____

____

____

____

ACTIVITY 5.4 COMMON CREDIT MYTHS

Time: 30 minutes

Materials: *Responsible Money* workbooks, name tags, flip chart, markers, pens or pencils

Objective:

To provide a better understanding of how credit works and to dispel some of the misinformation about credit.

Learning Competencies:

As a result of this session, the participants will be able to better identify common credit myths and better explain how the US credit system works.

Procedures:

The facilitator(s) will:

1. Explain that there are many misconceptions about credit. This activity will help separate fact from fiction.

2. Read or ask participants to read the first myth:

   Debit cards help build credit. *This is not true. Whether it is a prepaid card or a debit card from your local bank, debit cards do not report to the credit bureaus. Many people believe that by choosing the credit option at a store when they use a debit card, they are building credit history. This is not the case. The choice between debit and credit refers to how the transaction is processed. Debit transactions are treated more like cash and allow you to get cash back or receive cash for a returned item, while credit transactions are processed through Visa or MasterCard and give you buying protection from some types of fraud.*

3. Leave time to discuss each myth.

4. Ask questions like: "How many people thought this was true before today?"

5. Repeat this for the remaining four myths found on **page 53** of the *Responsible Money* workbook. The other myths include the following:

- **I must carry a balance on my credit card.** *Again, this is not true. Credit reports show payment history. Therefore, using your card every month and then paying it off by the due date will show a positive payment history and improve your score. Using your card and making on-time payments is what improves your score, not carrying a balance. In fact, carrying too high of a balance hurts your score.*
- **Prepaid cards are just like credit cards.** *Don't be fooled into thinking that a prepaid debit card is the same. Prepaid debit cards will not build your credit. Similar to a gift card, prepaid cards only subtract from money you have already spent. (Note: See Appendix 1 for definition.)*
- **I must pay to get my credit report.** *The fact is that there is a fee to receive the score, but you are able to receive your credit report free once per year. The official website to receive your report is www.annualcreditreport.com. According to the site, you will receive a report from all three national credit bureaus immediately, if requested online. Reports can also be processed by phone at (877) 322-8228 or by mail:*

  Annual Credit Report Request Service
  P.O. Box 105281
  Atlanta, GA 30348-5281

  Requests made by phone or through the mail will be sent within fifteen days. Watch out for websites that offer free credit scores. Many charge a monthly fee if you do not cancel your trial membership in time.
- **Payday or title loans can help credit.** *This is false. Most payday or title loan companies only report negative credit information. Stay away from these types of loans. On-time payments are rarely reported, but missing a lot of payments will result in a negative hit to your credit.*

6. Ask participants if they have any questions.

7. Ask for two volunteers to perform the skit below.

Scene 2

- **Character 1:** "Look what I just got. My very own credit card!"
- **Character 2:** "I thought the bank rejected your application?"
- **Character 1:** "Yeah, well, I found another way."
- **Character 2:** "This card says prepaid. That's not a credit card."
- **Character 1:** "I bought something today and they asked me if I wanted credit or debit. I chose credit and it worked."

8. Ask the participants to discuss the skit, analyzing the main problem with how Character 1 views credit.

ACTIVITY 5.5 IMPROVING YOUR CREDIT SCORE

Time: 30 minutes

Materials: *Responsible Money* workbooks, name tags, flip chart, markers, pens or pencils

Objective:

To provide a better understanding of how credit works and to provide tips on improving your credit score.

Learning Competencies:

As a result of this session, the participants will be able to:

1. Order their annual credit report.
2. Further explain how credit works.
3. Understand how to improve their credit score.

Procedures:

The facilitator(s) will:

1. Explain that having a good credit score has several benefits which include the following: lower interest rates, faster approval for renting apartments, approval for credit, better car insurance rates, no security deposit needed for utilities, and increased employment opportunities.
2. Read the six tips to improve credit found on **pages 54–55** of the *Responsible Money* workbook. These tips are as follows:
    - **Get a Credit Card.** *If you do not have a credit card, get one. If you have made some credit mistakes in the past and have found it difficult to get approved, consider getting a secured credit card. Secured cards require that you pay a security deposit. The larger the deposit, the larger your credit limit. When you make a purchase, the purchase subtracts from the available credit balance—not the security deposit. The security deposit is only used if the account goes into default. The lender would then close the account, subtract what you owe, and mail a*

check for the remaining balance of the original deposit. Whichever type of credit card you get, make sure it reports credit information to the three bureaus and pay the bill on time.

- **Pay Down Your Credit Cards.** *If you already have credit cards, pay them off. Credit scores improve when only a small percentage of your available balance is used. If possible, pay the entire balance at the end of every month. If you already carry a high balance, set a goal of getting the balance down to 25% of the total available balance. Paying more than the monthly minimum balance will help you achieve this goal.*
- **Dispute Old Problems.** *This tip can help your score the most. Review your credit report and dispute anything negative. Sometimes the lender will not bother sending a response because the amount was small or they can't find the records. The older and smaller the better. Credit bureaus may just take the item off the report. It takes effort to write each bureau, but it's worth it. (Note: Negative items stay on credit reports seven years after the resolution of the problem. Disputing old, unresolved debts can potentially raise credit scores hundreds of points, if old negative items are removed.)*
- **Get a Loan.** *Paying an installment-type loan will help your score. These include auto, student, personal, and home loans, to name a few. Showing a positive payment history for twenty-four months will help improve your score.*
- **Pay Your Bills on Time.** *This may seem simple, but certain bills must be paid on time. Many utility companies report late payments to credit bureaus. The logic behind this is that if a person will not pay on time to heat their home, why would they pay a credit card bill? Remember: creditors want their interest payments. When a person appears to struggle to pay for essentials like electricity and natural gas, creditors question whether they would get their payments if a line of credit were approved. Paying utility bills on time can improve your score, if the utility company reports payment history each month.*
- **Communicate.** *Do not duck and dodge the calls from creditors. Communicate with them and you may be surprised. Sometimes they will waive a late fee or remove*

a late payment from your history, if you ask. Work with them and they will work with you to develop a payment plan that works best for your situation.

ACTIVITY 5.6 CLOSURE AND REFLECTION

Time: 10 minutes

Materials: *Responsible Money* workbooks, name tags, flip chart, markers, pens or pencils, assessment handout

Objective:

To reflect on how credit works, to evaluate whether participants understand key concepts, and to bring the session to a close.

Learning Competencies:

Participants will be able to reflect on what they have learned and think about how they will use this information in their daily lives.

Procedures:

The facilitator(s) will:

1. Pass out the assessment handout.
2. Ask the participants to complete the following two questions.
    - Which of these is **not** one of the three major US credit bureaus?
        a. Egalite
        b. Equifax
        c. Experian
        d. TransUnion

      Correct Answer: a

    - What is a credit score?
        a. The amount of interest you pay annually using a credit card.
        b. A number representing a potential borrower's credit risk.
        c. A government system to rate banks.
        d. The money that lenders earn from letting people borrow money.

      Correct Answer: b

3. Tell the participants to complete the following “What I Learned” Log, found on **page 44** of the *Responsible Money* workbook.

"WHAT I LEARNED" LOG

Courtesy of rupixen.com via *Unsplash*.

One thing I learned today is:

____

____

____

____

____

On a scale of 0–5, how likely are you to use what you have learned in this session?

0 = Not at all likely 5 = Very likely

0 1 2 3 4 5

What I learned in this session will help me because:

____

____

____

____

____

____

____

____

Session 6
Responsible Investing

Description of Session:

This session will focus on understanding the basics of investing. This includes investments in stocks, mutual funds, retirement plans, and college savings plans.

Courtesy of Patrick Weissenberger via *Unsplash*.

Before the Session:

1. Gather needed materials including the following: *Responsible Money* workbooks for each participant, calculators, name tags, pens or pencils, flip chart, markers, and paper.

2. Make copies of post-test handout for all participants.

3. Write the name(s) of the facilitator(s) on the flip chart.

4. Hang up posters and visual aids.

ACTIVITY 6.1 WARM-UP

Time: 10 minutes

Materials: *Responsible Money* workbooks, name tags, flip chart, markers, pens or pencils

Objective:

To provide a better understanding of how participants feel about investing and to measure the group's level of prior knowledge.

Learning Competencies:

As a result of this session, the participants will be able to:

1. Identify their feelings about their past investments.
2. Evaluate the results of any past investments.
3. Discuss reasons they have not started investing.

Procedures:

The facilitator(s) will:

1. Greet the participants with a handshake as they enter the room.
2. Ask each participant to sign in and fill out a name tag.

The participants will:

1. Complete warm-up exercises 1–3 on **page 61** of the workbook. These exercises are as follows:
   - *To me, investing means:* ____________________
   - *The worst investment I ever made was:* ____________________
   - *The best investment I ever made was:* ____________________
2. Discuss the warm-up exercises.

3. Ask participants questions and allow time for discussion (e.g., "Why have you waited to start an investment plan? Have you ever purchased a stock? Have you ever invested in a mutual fund?").

ACTIVITY 6.2 FINANCIAL TERMS

Time: 20 minutes

Materials: *Responsible Money* workbooks, name tags, flip chart, markers, pens or pencils

Objective:

To provide a better understanding of several financial terms.

Learning Competencies:

As a result of this session, the participants will be able to:

1. Define several financial terms found on **page 62** of the *Responsible Money* workbook.

2. Discuss the benefits of compound interest and dollar cost averaging.

Procedures:

The facilitator(s) will:

1. Say: "There are a lot of terms associated with investing; it's almost like learning a new language. Therefore, we will discuss a few common financial terms, however the glossary found in Appendix 1 contains several more terms that may help."

2. Ask the participants: "What is a bull market? Or what does it mean to be bullish?"

   - **Answer:** A bull market is increasing in value. A bull is an investor who believes a stock will increase in value. This type of investor is bullish regarding a particular stock.

3. Ask the participants: "What is a bear market? Or what is a bear?"

   - **Answer:** A bear market is the opposite of a bull market; it is decreasing in value. A bear is an investor who believes a particular stock will decrease in value.

4. Ask the participants: "What is a stock? Or what does it mean to own stock?"

   - **Answer:** A stock is a type of security that allows investors to buy ownership shares in a company. Certain stockholders have voting rights and are entitled to vote at company shareholder meetings.

5. Read the other definitions found on **page 63** of the workbook, which are as follows:

   - **Blue Chip.** *A company that has a long, solid history of increased earnings. Companies like Coca-Cola® and McDonald's® fall into this category.*
   - **Bond.** *A type of security that allows investors to buy a company's debt. Bond investors loan money to the companies (issuers) with the promise of earning interest and repayment in the future.*
   - **Compound Interest.** *Interest that accrues on the initial deposit and the accumulated interest of that initial deposit. Compounding interest allows your money to grow at a much faster rate than simple interest by reinvesting earnings.*
   - **Dividend.** *A portion of a company's income paid to shareholders. Dividends are paid quarterly or annually.*
   - **Dollar Cost Averaging.** *The concept of allocating the same amount of money periodically (weekly, biweekly, or monthly) to purchase securities or other investments.*
   - **Mutual Fund.** *A type of security that allows the investor to buy fractions of company shares. Each share of a mutual fund is made up of stocks, bonds, or a mixture of both from many different companies.*

Notes

ACTIVITY 6.3 UNDERSTANDING THE RISKS

Time: 20 minutes

Materials: *Responsible Money* workbooks, calculators, name tags, flip chart, markers, pens or pencils

Objective:

To provide a better understanding of some of the risks associated with investing.

Learning Competencies:

As a result of this session, the participants will be able to:

1. Increase their capacity to discuss the risks involved with investing.
2. Become more familiar with other financial terms and concepts.

Procedures:

The facilitator(s) will:

1. Ask participants what they think about investment risk.
2. Allow time to discuss.
3. Write a few responses on the flip chart.
4. Discuss the idea that if there is no risk, then there is no reward (e.g., opening a small business). Investments work in the same way. Safe investments, like bank savings accounts and CDs, have almost no risk and they yield almost no return. Online savings accounts typically have slightly higher interest rates, but if you do not live or work close to a branch, you will have limited access to your money. Typically, the higher the risk potential, the higher the *potential* reward. Smart investors must learn to manage risk.
5. Read the following paragraph from **page 63** of the *Responsible Money* workbook:

   All investments come with risks. Anyone who says otherwise is not being honest. Therefore, it is important to understand any investment you make. Understanding the risks associated with different types of investments is the first step toward becoming an informed investor. Investment professionals are required to ask questions about risk tolerance. Here are a few investment risks you should consider before investing.

6. Read (or ask for volunteers to read) the following types of risk from **page 63** of the workbook.

    - **Loss of Principal.** *This is also known as market risk. Ask yourself if you can afford to lose the money you choose to invest. If the answer is no, decrease the amount or reconsider your investment. Discuss the possibility of loss with your financial professional. Some investments that have little risk of losing principal include treasury bills, annuities, and money market funds. Stocks, however, can gain or lose value quickly. It is important to understand the risks before you invest.*
    - **Liquidity.** *When will you need to get your money back? If you need the money to pay a property tax bill in six months, you should not tie it up in a long-term investment. It is important to understand if an investment is meant to be long-term or short-term.*
    - **Inflation.** *If you simply put your money under your mattress, there is risk. Besides the risk of theft or the money burning up in a fire, your money will not keep up with the rate of inflation. In 1940, the average cost for a new house was $3,920. Try buying a house for that today—that's not even enough for a down payment. Inflation is real and your investments should at least keep up with inflation.*

7. (Optional) State that there are other risks associated with investing, such as the following:

    - **Opportunity cost** is the risk of missing another investment opportunity.
    - **Currency risk** refers to the fact that if an investment is in another country, changes in their currency could affect the value of your investment.
    - **Taxability risk** is the risk that a tax-exempt investment could potentially lose that status.
    - **Credit risk** refers to the risk that a company that issues a bond will not repay. Typically, the higher the risk, the higher the interest rate on the bond.

ACTIVITY 6.4 DOLLAR COST AVERAGING

Time: 20 minutes

Materials: *Responsible Money* workbooks, calculators, name tags, flip chart, markers, pens or pencils

Objective:

To provide a better understanding of dollar cost averaging.

Learning Competencies:

As a result of this session, the participants will be able to:

1. Demonstrate an understanding of dollar cost averaging.
2. Describe the benefits of dollar cost averaging.

Procedures:

The facilitator(s) will:

1. Tell the participants to find the Dollar Cost Averaging Worksheet on **page 64** of the *Responsible Money* workbook.
2. Reread the definition of dollar cost averaging: "The concept of allocating the same amount of money periodically (weekly, biweekly, or monthly) to purchase securities or other investments."
3. Pass out calculators.
4. Ask the participants to answer the questions on the worksheet. (If needed, remind participants that a mathematical average is calculated by adding up the total amount and dividing that sum by the total number of entries.)
5. Allow participants time to complete the worksheet.
6. Ask the participants to share their answers.
7. Write the correct answers on the flip chart.
8. Allow time, if needed, for participants to make corrections.

9. Discuss the benefits of dollar cost averaging. Some of these benefits include:
    - The ability to budget the amount invested each month.
    - Lower average purchase price when compared to a one-time investment.
    - Lower average purchase price when compared to the average price of the investment.
    - A larger number of shares purchased when compared to a one-time investment.
10. State that the results on this worksheet are for illustration purposes only and do not reflect a particular investment.
11. Ask the following bonus question: "How much would the shares be worth on December 15, 2020?"
    - **Answer:** $927.28! A profit of $27.28 = 3.03% gain.

Dollar Cost Averaging Worksheet (and Answer Key)

Amount of Investment	Date of Investment	Cost Per Share	Number of Shares Bought
$75	January 15, 2020	$10.00	7.50
$75	February 15, 2020	$10.16	7.38
$75	March 15, 2020	$9.82	7.64
$75	April 15, 2020	$9.99	7.51
$75	May 15, 2020	$10.15	7.39
$75	June 15, 2020	$10.26	7.31
$75	July 15, 2020	$10.48	7.16
$75	August 15, 2020	$10.21	7.35
$75	September 15, 2020	$9.88	7.59
$75	October 15, 2020	$10.16	7.38
$75	November 15, 2020	$10.32	7.27
$75	December 15, 2020	$10.46	7.17

Use the above chart to answer the following questions:

1. How much money was invested over the course of the year?
    - **Answer:** $900.00
2. What was the average selling price for the stock?
    - **Answer:** $10.16

3. How many shares was the investor able to buy over the course of the year?

    - **Answer:** 88.65

4. What was the average price the investor paid for each share of stock?

    - **Answer:** $10.15

5. How many shares would the investor have been able to buy if he had saved his money and made a one-time investment on December 15?

    - **Answer:** 86.04

ACTIVITY 6.5 HOW TO INVEST

Time: 20 minutes

Materials: *Responsible Money* workbooks, name tags, flip chart, markers, pens or pencils

Objective:
To provide a better understanding of the questions to ask before making an investment.

Learning Competencies:
As a result of this session, the participants will be able to:

1. Understand how SIPC protects investors.

2. Identify various goals of investment instruments.

3. Address the misconception that only the wealthy can invest.

Procedures:
The facilitator(s) will:

1. Explain that this session will not give specific investment advice and that the facilitator is not a licensed financial professional. The goal of this session is to help the participants ask better questions, so that they will better understand any future investments.

2. Read the following tips from **page 65** of the *Responsible Money* workbook.

    - **Do Your Homework.** *Look for stable financial firms. Make sure your bank, investment firm, or financial website is a member of the Securities Investment Protection Corporation (SIPC), before you invest. The SIPC does not guarantee funds due to market changes or provide safety of principal like the FDIC because risk is part of the stock market. However, they can help recover money lost due to brokerage misconduct or failure. The SIPC can help individual investors recover up to $500,000 worth of missing securities. Go to www.sipc.org to learn more about how SIPC protects the rights of securities investors.*

- **Understand Your Investment.** *It is important to understand any investment you make. Investments have different goals. Some investments seek to provide the investor with income in the form of dividend or interest payments; other investments seek growth, while others seek safety. Make sure you understand your investments and that the goal of the investment matches your personal financial goals. Mutual funds have a prospectus that details the fund's goals and assets. Request and read an investment's prospectus before you invest. When buying stocks, invest in stable companies. Read about the company and, if you would not want to own the company, don't buy its stock.*
- **Start Small.** *Part of a successful investment strategy is dollar cost averaging because this allows you to include investments in your monthly budget. Once you have established an emergency savings fund, start putting money into an investment account. Most brokerages will allow some form of dollar cost averaging. If you can invest at least $25 a month, you can start an investment plan.*
- **Make It Automatic.** *Having to write a check and mail it in might prevent you from investing on a regular basis, so consider using automatic investment withdrawals from your checking or savings account. For best results, set up an automatic investment plan.*

Notes

ACTIVITY 6.6 INVESTING FOR RETIREMENT

Time: 20 minutes

Materials: *Responsible Money* workbooks, name tags, flip chart, markers, pens or pencils

Objective:
To provide a better understanding of investing for retirement.

Learning Competencies:
As a result of this session, the participants will be able to:

1. Explain the benefit of compound interest.

2. Become more aware of the importance of saving for retirement.

Procedures:
The facilitator(s) will:

1. Ask participants: "How many people here are over 55?"

2. Say: "The future of Social Security is in doubt. The unpredictability of government legislation suggests that people currently under the age of 55 should plan on receiving reduced levels of social security when they become eligible, if they receive benefits at all. Therefore, it is more important than ever to save for retirement."

3. Read the following tip from **page 66** of the *Responsible Money* workbook.

   Getting Started. *You can never save too much money. Whether you believe it or not, you may get old one day and, when you do, it would be nice to have a little money to enjoy your golden years. Younger investors have the benefit of time; they can put small amounts of money away over a longer period. However, older investors must save more, if they want to retire well. Most retirement plans allow investors over 55 years of age to contribute higher amounts than younger investors. The longer your time horizon, the more compound interest your money will earn. Whatever your situation, getting started is the most important step. Figure 6.1 below illustrates the power of compounding interest. Over time,* *the value of an account can increase greatly because of compound interest and the money in a retirement account grows tax-free.*

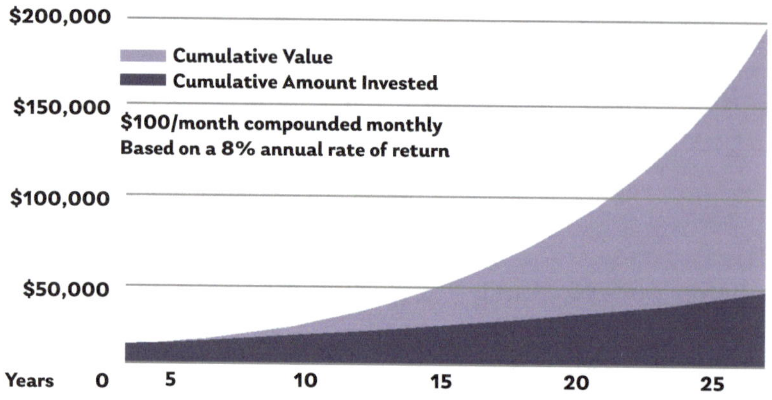

Figure 6.1: The Power of Compound Interest courtesy of Matthew Wright

4. Read the disclaimer under the figure as follows:

   These returns do not represent the past or future results of any specific financial investment and are for illustrative purposes only. This example assumes that all earnings are reinvested, without taking into account any fees, taxes, or expenses. Investing does not guarantee a profit or protect against loss. Investors should consider the risks and analyze their ability to invest during periods of market decline.

5. Explain that this disclaimer represents a common one you will see from investment firms.

6. Allow time for participants to discuss Figure 6.1.

7. Read the next tip found on **page 66** of the workbook.

   Choosing the Right Plan. *If you have an income, you can and should contribute to a retirement plan. Start by looking at your employer's retirement plan benefits. If your company matches any part of your contributions, join the plan—it's the same as being paid more money. If you don't have a retirement plan at work, you can always start an Individual Retirement Account, known as an IRA. The main types include the Traditional IRA and the Roth IRA.*

8. Explain how the decision of which plan to choose is not as important as the decision to get started. Remember that small amounts of money add up. Also, retirement dollars are meant for use at retirement, so the IRS penalizes early withdrawals (with a few exceptions).

ACTIVITY 6.7 SAVING FOR COLLEGE

Time: 20 minutes

Materials: *Responsible Money* workbooks, name tags, flip chart, markers, pens or pencils

Objective:

To provide a better understanding of the two most common types of college savings and investment plans.

Learning Competencies:

As a result of this session, the participants will be able to:

1. Identify the two most popular types of college savings and investment plans.

2. Compare and contrast the benefits of both the Coverdell ESA and 529 plans.

Procedures:

The facilitator(s) will:

1. Read the following excerpt from **page 67** of the *Responsible Money* workbook:

   Saving for retirement is more important than saving for college. After all, there are no scholarships, grants, or loans to help you in retirement. Therefore, saving for college should not replace saving for your retirement. However, sending a loved one to school with some money (and receiving some tax benefits while doing it) would be ideal. Here are some plans that may help.

   - **529 Plans.** *Section 529 of the IRS code allows states and educational institutions to establish savings or investment plans to help make it easier to save for college. These plans have tax benefits and are meant for future college expenses for a child or grandchild. There are two types: prepaid tuition plans and savings plans. Withdrawals for college expenses are tax-free. Federal law also allows families to use up to $10,000 for K–12 tuition without taxes or penalties. Some related expenses* *include tuition, fees, books, room and board, and even computers. The contributor maintains control of the account regardless of the beneficiary's age. In short, 529 plans are the property of the parent or other contributor who created the account. Since their creation in 1996, 529 plans have become a popular choice for college savings.*

- **Coverdell ESA Plans.** *Coverdell ESA plans also receive tax benefits, including tax-free distributions for school expenses, just like 529 plans. However, these plans differ in several ways. First, Coverdell ESA plans are the property of the student. This can reduce their financial aid package options and limit your control of the money when the minor turns 18. Funds in a Coverdell ESA plan can be used for private elementary and secondary school costs. Furthermore, the Coverdell ESA's maximum yearly contribution is $2,000, but you can contribute significantly more to a 529 plan each year.*
- **UTMA/UGMA Accounts.** *UTMA (Uniform Transfers to Minors Act) and UGMA (Uniform Gifts to Minors Act) are types of custodial accounts that allow parents and others to help save for a child's future. They provide more flexibility because the funds are not limited to school expenses. However, they provide no tax benefits and become the property of the child at a certain age, depending on the state in which you live (typically 18 or 21).*

These plans come with pros and cons. The good news is that if you start a Coverdell ESA plan and change your mind, you can transfer it to a 529 plan without penalty; but this is not true the other way around. Also, the plans can be used at the same time for the same child. If you contribute the maximum amount to a Coverdell and still want to save more for college, you could make additional contributions to a 529 plan. As with any investment, there are risks; so consult a licensed financial professional for specific financial advice.

2. (Optional) Use the flip chart to create a comparison chart between 529 and Coverdell accounts. Here is an example:

Highlights	Coverdell ESA	Prepaid 529	529 Savings Plan
Contribution Limit	$2,000	Higher limit: Depends on the plan	Higher limit: Depends on the plan
Qualified Expenses	Eligible K–12 and college expenses such as tuition, books, and uniforms.	Prepay tuition at certain participating colleges, but not available in most states. Only covers tuition and fees.	Up to full college tuition. Limited to $10,000 per year for K–12 tuition. Other qualified expenses for college only and includes supplies, internet access, and more.
Tax Benefits	Not deductible; funds grow tax deferred; beneficiary does not pay taxes on qualified withdrawals.	Not deductible; may be deductible at the state level; funds grow tax-deferred; tax-free distribution for college expenses.	Not deductible; may be deductible at the state level; funds grow tax-deferred; tax-free distribution for college expenses.
Ownership	Student owns account at 18.	Remains in the control of the giver.	Remains in the control of the giver.
Effect on Financial Aid	Owned by the student, assets are considered in financial aid.	Because owned by the contributor, has only a small effect on financial aid.	Because owned by the contributor, has only a small effect on financial aid.

Sources:

- "Tax Benefits for Education," IRS (www.irs.gov/uac/Tax-Benefits-for-Education:-Information-Center).
- The Motley Fool (www.fool.com).

ACTIVITY 6.8 CLOSURE AND REFLECTION

Time: 10 minutes

Materials: *Responsible Money* workbooks, name tags, flip chart, markers, pens or pencils, post-test handout

Objective:

To reflect on how various investments work, to evaluate whether participants understand key concepts, and to bring the session to a close.

Learning Competencies:

Participants will be able to reflect on what they have learned and think about how they will use this information in their daily lives.

Procedures:

The facilitator(s) will:

1. Ask the participants to answer the following two questions.

   - Dollar cost averaging helps investors because:
     a. They can budget how much they want to invest.
     b. It lowers the average cost of the investment.
     c. It guarantees you will make money.
     d. Both a & b.
     e. None of the above.

   Correct Answer: d

   - ______________________ allow(s) your money to grow at a much faster rate than simple interest.
     a. Dividends.
     b. Dollar cost averaging.
     c. Compound interest.
     d. Inflation.
     e. None of the above.

   Correct Answer: c

2. Ask participants to complete the "What I Learned" Log on **page 68** of the *Responsible Money* workbook, as follows:

"WHAT I LEARNED" LOG

Courtesy of Patrick Weissenberger via *Unsplash*.

One thing I learned today is:

____

____

____

____

____

On a scale of 0–5, how likely are you to use what you have learned in this session?

0 = Not at all likely 5 = Very likely

0 1 2 3 4 5

What I learned in this session will help me because:

____

____

____

____

____

____

3. Pass out the post-test handout.

4. Ask participants to complete the post-test handout.

Notes

Appendix 1: Glossary

GLOSSARY

- **Account History.** The payment history of an account over a specific period of time, including the number of times the account was past due or over limit.
- **Annual Percentage Rate (APR).** The cost of credit on a yearly basis, expressed as a percentage.
- **Annual Percentage Yield (APY).** A percentage rate reflecting the total amount of interest paid on a deposit account based on the interest rate and the frequency of compounding for a 365-day year.
- **Annuity.** A life insurance contract sold by insurance companies, brokers, and other financial institutions. It is usually sold as a retirement investment. An annuity is a long-term investment and can have steep surrender charges and penalties for withdrawal before the annuity's maturity date. (Annuities are not FDIC-insured.)
- **Ask Price.** The lowest price that a seller will accept when selling a stock.
- **Automated Clearing House (ACH).** A computerized facility used by member depository institutions to electronically combine, sort, and distribute inter-bank credits and debits. ACHs process electronic transfers of government securities and provide customer services, such as direct deposit of customers' salaries and government benefit payments (i.e., social security, welfare, and veterans' entitlements), as well as preauthorized transfers.
- **Automatic Bill Payment.** A checkless system for paying recurring bills with one authorization statement to a financial institution. For example, the customer would only have to provide one authorization form/letter/document to pay the cable bill each month. The necessary debits and credits are made through an Automated Clearing House (ACH).
- **Availability Date.** The date when funds deposited into a bank account will be available for withdrawal.
- **Availability Policy.** Bank's policy as to when funds deposited into an account will be available for withdrawal.
- **Available Balance.** The balance of an account less any hold, uncollected funds, and restrictions against the account.
- **Balance Transfer.** The process of moving an outstanding balance from one credit card to another. This is usually done to obtain

a lower interest rate on the outstanding balance. Transfers are sometimes subjected to a balance transfer fee.

- **Bank Statement.** Periodically, the bank provides a statement of a customer's deposit account. It shows all deposits made, all checks paid, and other debits posted during the period (usually one month), as well as the current balance.
- **Bankrupt.** A bankrupt person, firm, or corporation has insufficient assets to cover their debts. The debtor seeks relief through a court proceeding to work out a payment schedule or to erase debts. In some cases, the debtor must surrender control of all assets to a court-appointed trustee.
- **Bankruptcy.** The legal proceedings by which the affairs of a bankrupt person are turned over to a trustee or receiver for administration under the bankruptcy laws. There are two types of bankruptcy:

    a. Involuntary bankruptcy: One or more creditors of an insolvent debtor file a petition having the debtor declared bankrupt.

    b. Voluntary bankruptcy: The debtor files a petition claiming inability to meet financial obligations and willingness to be declared bankrupt.

- **Bear.** An investor who thinks the market or a particular stock will decrease in value.
- **Beneficiary.** A person who is entitled to receive the benefits or proceeds of a will, trust, insurance policy, retirement plan, annuity, or other contract.
- **Bid Price.** The highest price an investor will pay for a particular stock.
- **Blue Chip.** A company that has a long, solid history of increased earnings. Companies like Coca-Cola® and McDonald's® fall into this category.
- **Bond.** A type of security that allows investors to buy a company's debt. Bond investors loan money to the companies (issuers) with the promise of earning interest and repayment in the future.
- **Bond, US Savings.** Different from a bond security, US savings bonds are issued in face value denominations by the US Government in denominations ranging from $50 to $10,000. They are typically long-term, low-risk investment tools.
- **Bull.** An investor who thinks the market or a particular stock will increase in value. The opposite of a bear.

- **Cashier's Check.** A check drawn on the funds of the bank, not against the funds in a depositor's account. However, the depositor pays for the cashier's check with funds from their account. The primary benefit of a cashier's check is that the recipient of the check is assured that the funds are available.
- **Certificate of Deposit (CD).** A negotiable instrument issued by a bank in exchange for funds, usually bearing interest, deposited with the bank.
- **Charge-off.** The balance on a credit obligation that a lender no longer expects to be repaid and writes off as a bad debt.
- **Check 21 Act.** Check 21 is a federal law designed to enable banks to handle more checks electronically, which is intended to make check processing faster and more efficient. Check 21 is the short name for the Check Clearing for the 21st Century Act, which went into effect on October 28, 2004.
- **ChexSystems.** The ChexSystems, Inc. network is comprised of member financial institutions that regularly contribute information on mishandled checking and savings accounts to a central location. ChexSystems shares this information among member institutions to help them assess the risk of opening new accounts. ChexSystems only shares information with the member institutions; it does not decide on new account openings. Generally, information remains on ChexSystems for five years.
- **Collection Agency.** A company hired by a creditor to collect a debt that is owed. Creditors typically hire a collection agency only after they have made efforts to collect the debt themselves, usually through letters and telephone calls.
- **Compound Interest.** Interest that accrues on the initial deposit and the accumulated interest of that initial deposit. Compounding interest allows your money to grow at a much faster rate than simple interest.
- **Consumer Credit Counseling Service.** A service which specializes in working with consumers who are overextended with debts and need to make arrangements with creditors.
- **Consumer Reporting Agency.** An agency that regularly collects or evaluates individual consumer credit information or other information about consumers and sells consumer reports for a fee to creditors or others. Typical clients include banks, mortgage lenders, credit card companies, and other financing companies.
- **Coverdell Education Savings Account (ESA).** A tax-advantaged investment account that encourages saving for future educational

expenses. The funds from an ESA can be used for primary, secondary, or college expenses.

- **Credit Bureau.** An agency that collects individual credit information and sells it for a fee to creditors so they can decide whether to grant a loan. Typical clients include banks, mortgage lenders, credit card companies, and other financing companies. Also commonly referred to as a consumer reporting agency or a credit reporting agency.
- **Credit Card.** A card issued by a financial company giving the holder an option to borrow funds, usually at point of sale. Credit cards charge interest and are primarily used for short-term financing. Interest usually begins one month after a purchase is made and borrowing limits are pre-set according to the individual's credit rating.
- **Credit Report.** A detailed report of an individual's credit history prepared by a credit bureau and used by a lender to determine a loan applicant's creditworthiness.
- **Credit Score.** A number, roughly between 300 and 850, that measures an individual's credit worthiness. The most well-known type of credit score is the FICO® score. This score represents the answer from a mathematical formula that assigns numerical values to various pieces of information in your credit report.
- **Cut-off Time.** A time of day established by a bank for receipt of deposits. After the cut-off time, deposits are considered received on the next banking day.
- **Debit.** A debit may be an account entry representing money you owe a lender or money that has been taken from your deposit account.
- **Debit Card.** A debit card allows the account owner to access their funds electronically. Debit cards may be used to obtain cash from automated teller machines or to purchase goods or services using point-of-sale systems. The use of a debit card involves immediate debiting and crediting of consumers' accounts.
- **Debt Collector.** Any person who regularly collects debts owed to others.
- **Debt-to-Income Ratio (DTI).** The percentage of a consumer's monthly gross income that goes toward paying debts. Generally, the higher the ratio, the higher the perceived risk. Loans with higher risk are generally priced at a higher interest rate.
- **Deposit Slip.** An itemized memorandum of the cash and other funds that a customer presents to the bank for credit to his or her account.

- **Direct Deposit.** A payment that is electronically deposited into an individual's account at a depository institution.
- **Disclosures.** Certain information that federal and state laws require creditors to give to borrowers, relative to the terms of the credit extended.
- **Dividend.** A portion of a company's income paid to shareholders. Dividends are paid quarterly or annually.
- **Dollar Cost Averaging.** The concept of allocating the same amount of money periodically (weekly, biweekly, or monthly) to purchase securities or other investments.
- **Dow Jones Industrial Average (DJIA).** A list of thirty blue chip companies, often used as a gauge for the entire stock market. Commonly referred to as the Dow.
- **Electronic Funds Transfer (EFT).** The transfer of money between accounts by consumer electronic systems—such as automated teller machines (ATMs) and electronic payment of bills—rather than by check or cash. (Wire transfers, checks, drafts, and paper instruments do not fall into this category.)
- **Federal Deposit Insurance Corporation (FDIC).** A government corporation that insures the deposits of all national and state banks that are members of the Federal Reserve System.
- **Federal Reserve System.** The central bank of the United States. The Fed, as it is commonly called, regulates the US monetary and financial system. The Federal Reserve System is composed of a central governmental agency in Washington, DC (the Board of Governors) and twelve regional Federal Reserve Banks in major cities throughout the United States.
- **FICO® Score.** A type of credit score that makes up a large portion of the credit report that lenders use to assess an applicant's credit risk and whether to extend a loan. FICO® is an acronym for the Fair Isaac Corporation, the creators of the FICO® score. The FICO® score is the most commonly used credit score.
- **Finance Charge.** The total cost of credit a customer must pay on a consumer loan, including interest. The Truth in Lending Act requires disclosure of the finance charge.
- **Financial Market.** Often referred to as the market, the financial market is the mechanism that allows people to buy and sell (trade) financial securities such as stock and bonds.
- **Float.**

    a. The amount of uncollected funds, represented by checks, in the possession of one bank but drawn on other banks.

b. The time that elapses between the day a check is deposited and the day it is presented for payment to the financial institution on which it is drawn.

- **Fraud Alert.** A key provision of the Fair and Accurate Credit Transactions Act of 2003 is the consumer's ability to place a fraud alert on their credit record. A consumer would use this option if they believed they were a victim of identity theft. The alert requires any creditor who is asked to extend credit to contact the consumer by phone and verify that the credit application was not made by an identity thief.
- **Frozen Account.** An account on which funds may not be withdrawn until a lien is satisfied and a court order or other legal process makes the account available for withdrawal.
- **Hold.** Used to indicate that a certain amount of a customer's balance may not be withdrawn until an item has been collected or until a specific check or debit has posted.
- **Insufficient Funds.** When a depositor's checking account balance is inadequate to pay a check presented for payment.
- **Interest.** The term interest is used to describe the cost of using money.
- **Kiting.** Writing a check in an amount that will overdraw the account, but making up the deficiency by depositing another check from another bank. For example, mailing a check for the mortgage when your checking account has insufficient funds to cover the check, but counting on receiving and depositing your paycheck before the mortgage company presents the check for payment.
- **Maturity.** The date on which the principal balance of a loan, bond, or other financial instrument becomes due and payable.
- **Minimum Balance.** The amount of money required to be on deposit in an account to qualify the depositor for special services or to waive a service charge.
- **Money Market Deposit Account.** A savings account that offers a higher rate of interest in exchange for larger-than-normal deposits. Insured by the FDIC, these accounts have limits on the number of transactions allowed and may require higher balances to receive the higher rate of interest.
- **Mutual Fund.** A type of security that allows the investor to buy fractions of company shares. Each share of a mutual fund is made up of stocks, bonds, or a mixture of both from many different companies.

- **P/E Ratio.** The ratio between stock price and a company's earnings is the P/E ratio. For example, a company that earned $2 per share of stock and has a share price of $20 has a P/E of 10.
- **Prepaid Credit Card.** A card issued by a financial institution that is preloaded with funds and is used like a normal credit card. A prepaid credit card works in the opposite way of a normal credit card, because instead of buying something with borrowed funds (through credit), you buy things with funds that have already been paid. This card functions like a gift card.
- **Prospectus.** A formal legal document, which is required by and filed with the Securities and Exchange Commission, that provides details about an investment offering for sale to the public. A prospectus should contain the facts an investor needs to make an informed investment decision.
- **Service Charge.** A charge assessed by a depository institution for processing transactions and maintaining accounts.
- **Stock.** A type of security that allows investors to buy ownership shares in a company. Certain stockholders have voting rights and are entitled to vote at company shareholder meetings.

Sources:

- Office of the Comptroller of the Currency (www.helpwithmybank.gov/dictionary/index-dictionary.html).
- *Investopedia* (www.investopedia.com/terms).

Appendix 2: Pre- & Post-test

PRE-TEST BUDGETING AND FINANCIAL OUTCOME MEASURES

Name ____________________

ID# ____________________

Date ____________________

Please read each statement or question carefully, then either place a checkmark next to your answer, circle "true" or "false," or circle the multiple-choice response.

1. Which of these is **not** one of the three major US credit bureaus?

   a. Equifax
   b. Experian
   c. Egalite
   d. TransUnion

2. The Latte Factor® is a term that refers to:

   a. The importance of saving small amounts of money over time.
   b. Cutting out unneeded routine purchases and saving that money.
   c. A boycott on buying coffee.
   d. I'm not sure.
   e. Both a & b.

3. Revenue and expenses are related because:

   a. As revenue increases, expenses also increase.
   b. As expenses decrease, revenue increases.
   c. As expenses decrease, revenue decreases.
   d. There is no relation between revenue and expenses.
   e. I'm not sure.

4. Volunteer work has several benefits, including:

   a. A chance to get references.

b. Work experience.
c. Networking opportunities.
d. Potential employment.
e. All of the above.

5. Dollar cost averaging helps investors because:
   a. They can budget how much they want to invest.
   b. It lowers the average cost of the investment.
   c. It guarantees you will make money.
   d. Both a and b.
   e. None of the above.

6. Which of the following is **not** considered when calculating your FICO® score?
   a. Your payment history.
   b. The types of credit you are using.
   c. The amount of debt you owe.
   d. Your income.
   e. All the above are considered.

7. Resumes today are:
   a. Often pre-screened by computers for key words and phrases.
   b. Thrown in the garbage immediately.
   c. Never pre-screened.
   d. Unnecessary.
   e. All of the above.

8. ______________________ allow(s) your money to grow at a much faster rate than simple interest.
   a. Dividends.
   b. Dollar cost averaging.
   c. Compound interest.
   d. Inflation.
   e. None of the above.

9. What is a credit score?

    a. The amount of interest you pay annually using a credit card.
    b. A number representing a potential borrower's credit risk.
    c. A government system to rate banks.
    d. The money that lenders earn from letting people borrow money.
    e. None of the above.

10. The benefits of banking include all the following **except**:

    a. Earning interest.
    b. Guaranteed loan approval.
    c. Avoiding check-cashing fees.
    d. Safety.
    e. None of the above.

11. The six steps to budgeting include all **except**:

    a. Accountability.
    b. Keeping it simple.
    c. Making more money.
    d. Knowing what you earn.
    e. Knowing what you spend.

12. A bank can place an extended hold on funds for all the following **except**:

    a. Frequent overdrafts
    b. Redeposited checks
    c. Random account holds
    d. New accounts
    e. Suspicious activity

13. What is the most commonly used credit score?

    a. FICO® score
    b. VantageScore
    c. Dunn & Bradstreet
    d. Acme credit score
    e. Amex score

14. Lenders use credit scores when deciding to extend which type of credit?

a. Mortgages
b. Personal loans
c. Credit cards
d. Auto loans
e. All of the above.

15. You can improve your credit score by having negative, incorrect information removed from your credit report.

True False

16. Prepaid credit cards can help build your credit history.

True False

17. To invest in the stock market, you need at least $1,000.

True False

18. When you write a check, it takes two days to clear the bank.

True False

POST-TEST BUDGETING AND FINANCIAL OUTCOME MEASURES

Name ________________________________

ID# ________________________________

Date ________________________________

Please read each statement or question carefully, then either place a checkmark next to your answer, circle "true" or "false," or circle the multiple-choice response.

AS A RESULT OF COMPLETING THIS CLASS

THE FOLLOWING QUESTIONS WILL ASSESS YOUR KNOWLEDGE ABOUT FINANCIAL MATTERS.

1. Which of these is **not** one of the three major US credit bureaus?
   a. Equifax
   b. Experian
   c. Egalite
   d. TransUnion
   e. I'm not sure.

2. Revenue and expenses are related because:
   a. As revenue increases, expenses also increase.
   b. As expenses decrease, revenue increases.
   c. As expenses decrease, revenue decreases.
   d. There is no relation between revenue and expenses.
   e. I'm not sure.

3. Which of the following is **not** considered when calculating your FICO® score?
   a. Your payment history.
   b. The types of credit you are using.

c. The amount of debt you owe.
d. Your income.
e. All of the above are considered.

4. Resumes today are:

a. Often pre-screened by computers for key words and phrases.
b. Thrown in the garbage immediately.
c. Never pre-screened.
d. Unnecessary.
e. All of the above.

5. ________________________ allow(s) your money to grow at a much faster rate than simple interest.

a. Dividends.
b. Dollar cost averaging.
c. Compound interest.
d. Inflation.
e. None of the above.

6. What is a credit score?

a. The amount of interest you pay annually using a credit card.
b. A number representing a potential borrower's credit risk.
c. A government system to rate banks.
d. The money that lenders earn from letting people borrow money.
e. None of the above.

7. The benefits of banking include all the following **except:**

a. Earning interest.
b. Guaranteed loan approval.
c. Avoiding check-cashing fees.
d. Safety.
e. None of the above.

8. Which of the following is **not** a reason a bank would place an extended hold on funds?

    a. Frequent overdrafts
    b. Redeposited checks
    c. Random account holds
    d. New accounts
    e. Suspicious activity

9. What is the most commonly used credit score?

    a. FICO® score
    b. VantageScore
    c. Dunn & Bradstreet
    d. Acme credit score
    e. Amex score

10. Lenders use credit scores to make approval decisions for which type of credit?

    a. Mortgages
    b. Personal loans
    c. Credit cards
    d. Auto loans
    e. All of the above.

11. You can improve your credit score by having negative, incorrect information removed from your credit report.

    True False

12. Prepaid credit cards can help build your credit history.

    True False

13. To invest in the stock market, you need at least $1,000.

    True False

14. When you write a check, it takes two days to clear the bank.

    True False

15. The Latte Factor® is a term that refers to:

a. The importance of saving small amounts of money over time.
b. Cutting out unneeded routine purchases and saving that money.
c. A boycott on buying coffee.
d. Both a & b.

16. Volunteer work has several benefits, including:

a. A chance to get references.
b. Work experience.
c. Networking opportunities.
d. Potential employment.
e. All of the above.

17. Dollar cost averaging helps investors because:

a. It lowers the average cost of the investment.
b. They can budget how much they want to invest.
c. It guarantees that you will make money.
d. Both a and b.
e. None of the above.

18. The six steps to budgeting include all **except**:

a. Accountability.
b. Keeping it simple.
c. Making more money.
d. Knowing what you earn.
e. Knowing what you spend.

POST-TEST KEY BUDGETING AND FINANCIAL OUTCOME MEASURES

Name ______________________________

ID# ______________________________

Date ______________________________

Please read each statement or question carefully, then either place a checkmark next to your answer, circle "true" or "false," or circle the multiple-choice response.

AS A RESULT OF COMPLETING THIS CLASS

THE FOLLOWING QUESTIONS WILL ASSESS YOUR KNOWLEDGE ABOUT FINANCIAL MATTERS.

1. Which of these is **not** one of the three major US credit bureaus?
   a. Equifax
   b. Experian
   c. **Egalite**
   d. TransUnion
   e. I'm not sure.

2. Revenue and expenses are related because:
   a. As revenue increases, expenses also increase.
   b. **As expenses decrease, revenue increases.**
   c. As expenses decrease, revenue decreases.
   d. There is no relation between revenue and expenses.
   e. I'm not sure.

3. Which of the following is **not** considered when calculating your FICO® score?
   a. Your payment history.
   b. The types of credit you are using.

c. The amount of debt you owe.
d. **Your income.**
e. All of the above are considered.

4. Resumes today are:

   a. **Often pre-screened by computers for key words and phrases.**
   b. Thrown in the garbage immediately.
   c. Never pre-screened.
   d. Unnecessary.
   e. All of the above.

5. ________________________ allow(s) your money to grow at a much faster rate than simple interest.

   a. Dividends.
   b. Dollar cost averaging.
   c. **Compound interest.**
   d. Inflation.
   e. None of the above.

6. What is a credit score?

   a. The amount of interest you pay annually using a credit card.
   b. **A number representing a potential borrower's credit risk.**
   c. A government system to rate banks.
   d. The money that lenders earn from letting people borrow money.
   e. None of the above.

7. The benefits of banking include all the following except:

   a. Earning interest.
   b. **Guaranteed loan approval.**
   c. Avoiding check-cashing fees.
   d. Safety.
   e. None of the above.

8. Which of the following is **not** a reason a bank would place an extended hold on funds?

   a. Frequent overdrafts
   b. Redeposited checks
   c. **Random account holds**
   d. New accounts
   e. Suspicious activity

9. What is the most commonly used credit score?

   a. **FICO® score**
   b. VantageScore
   c. Dunn & Bradstreet
   d. Acme credit score
   e. Amex score

10. Lenders use credit scores to make approval decisions for which type of credit?

    a. Mortgages
    b. Personal loans
    c. Credit cards
    d. Auto loans
    e. **All of the above.**

11. You can improve your credit score by having negative, incorrect information removed from your credit report.

    True False

12. Prepaid credit cards can help build your credit history.

    True **False**

13. To invest in the stock market, you need at least $1,000.

    True **False**

14. When you write a check, it takes two days to clear the bank.

    True **False**

15. The Latte Factor® is a term that refers to:

a. The importance of saving small amounts of money over time.
b. Cutting out unneeded routine purchases and saving that money.
c. A boycott on buying coffee.
d. **Both a & b.**

16. Volunteer work has several benefits, including:

a. A chance to get references.
b. Work experience.
c. Networking opportunities.
d. Potential employment.
e. **All of the above.**

17. Dollar cost averaging helps investors because:

a. It lowers the average cost of the investment.
b. They can budget how much they want to invest.
c. It guarantees that you will make money.
d. **Both a & b.**
e. None of the above.

18. The six steps to budgeting include all **except**:

a. Accountability.
b. Keeping it simple.
c. **Making more money.**
d. Knowing what you earn.
e. Knowing what you spend.

Appendix 3:
Financial Literacy Standards Map

RESPONSIBLE MONEY FINANCIAL LITERACY STANDARDS MAP

The Responsible Money Financial Literacy program offers six sessions that include activities and resources for you and your participants. This map will help you identify and select lessons to support the following standards:

- Common Core State Standards in Mathematics (CCSS)
- Council for Economic Education (CEE)®
- Jump$tart® Coalition for Personal Financial Literacy
- C3 Framework for Social Studies State Standards
- Family and Consumer Sciences National Standards

1. **"What Money Means to You" overview:** Learners identify their beliefs and values about money, while they explore the idea of wants vs. needs.

***Responsible Money* resource**	**CCSS in Mathematics**	**CEE® Standards**	**Jump$tart® Standards**	**C3 Framework for Social Studies**	**Family and Consumer Sciences National Standards**
Activity 1.2: What Money Means to You		Earning Income 2			Consumer & Family Resources 2.1.2
Activity 1.3: Ways We Use Our Money	6.NS.B.3 6.RP.A.3.C	Buying Goods and Services 1	Financial Decision Making Standard 1	Economics D2.Eco.1.6-8	Consumer & Family Resources 2.1.2

2. **"Sources of Money" overview:** Participants will explore their feelings about earning money, establish career goals, and explore the pros and cons of various ways for earning money.

***Responsible Money* resource**	**CCSS in Mathematics**	**CEE® Standards**	**Jump$tart® Standards**	**C3 Framework for Social Studies**	**Family and Consumer Sciences National Standards**
Activity 2.1: Warm-up			Employment and Income Standard 1		Career, Community & Family Connections 1.3.1
Activity 2.2: Pitfalls of Fast Money	6.NS.C.5	Earning Income 7,8	Financial Decision Making Standard 1,2&4	Economics D2.Eco.1.6-8	Consumer & Family Resources 2.1.2 2.5.1
Activity 2.3: Pros and Cons		Earning Income 2,3	Financial Decision Making Standard 4	Economics D2.Eco.2.9-12	Consumer & Family Resources 2.1.2
Activity 2.4: Finding Employment		Earning Income 2,3,4,5	Employment and Income Standard 1		Career Community and Family Connections 1.2.1 2.7.2

3. **"Budgeting and Saving" overview:** Participants are provided with strategies to begin budgeting and saving money.

Responsible Money **resource**	**CCSS in Mathematics**	**CEE® Standards**	**Jump$tart® Standards**	**C3 Framework for Social Studies**	**Family and Consumer Sciences National Standards**
Activity 3.2: Budgeting Tips		Buying Goods and Services 5,6	Financial Decision Making Standard 4	Economics D2.Eco.1.6-8	Consumer & Family Resources 2.1.2 2.6.2
Activity 3.3: Creating a Budget	6.NS.B.3	Buying Goods and Services 5,6	Spending and Saving Standard 1&4	Economics D2.Eco.2.6-8	Consumer & Family Resources 2.7.3
Activity 3.4: Saving Money	6.RP.A.3.C	Saving 7	Spending and Saving Standard 1&4		Consumer & Family Resources 2.7.6
Activity 3.5: US Savings Statistics	6.SP.B.4 7.SP.B.3	Saving 1	Spending and Saving Standard 4	Economics D2.Eco.10.9-12	Consumer & Family Resources 2.5.2

4. **"Personal Banking" overview:** This session focuses on understanding banking terms and account types, the benefits of banking, and avoiding common banking mistakes.

Responsible Money **resource**	**CCSS in Mathematics**	**CEE® Standards**	**Jump$tart® Standards**	**C3 Framework for Social Studies**	**Family and Consumer Sciences National Standards**
Activity 4.2: Banking Scenarios		Saving 1	Spending and Saving Standard 3	Economics D2.Eco.9.6-8	Consumer & Family Resources 2.6.4
Activity 4.3: Banking Terms		Saving 1,2,9	Spending and Saving Standard 3	Economics D2.Eco.9.9-12	Consumer & Family Resources 2.7.1
Activity 4.4: Common Banking Concerns		Saving 1	Spending and Saving Standard 3	Economics D2.Eco.9.9-12	Consumer & Family Resources 2.7.6
Activity 4.5: Benefits of Banking	6.NS.B.3	Saving 1.2,4,5	Spending and Saving Standard 3	Economics D2.Eco.9.9-12	Consumer & Family Resources 2.6.1

5. **"Understanding Credit" overview:** This session focuses on understanding how credit works, while discussing common misconceptions and tips for improving personal credit scores.

Responsible Money **resource**	**CCSS in Mathematics**	**CEE® Standards**	**Jump$tart® Standards**	**C3 Framework for Social Studies**	**Family and Consumer Sciences National Standards**
Activity 5.2: How Credit Works		Using Credit 1	Credit and Debt 1	D2.Eco.10.6-8	Consumer Services 3.3.3
Activity 5.3: Credit Terms		Using Credit 1,3,4,5,7,8	Credit and Debt 1,2	D2.Eco.10.6-8	Consumer Services 3.3.3
Activity 5.4: Common Credit Myths		Using Credit 3,4,5	Credit and Debt 1,2,3	D2.Eco.10.6-8	Consumer Services 3.3.3 3.3.8
Activity 5.5: Improving Your Credit Score	6.RP.A.3.C	Using Credit 6,7,8,9	Credit and Debt 1,2,3	D2.Eco.10.6-8	Consumer Services 3.3.3 3.3.8 Consumer & Family Resources 2.7.4

6. **"Responsible Investing" overview:** This session focuses on the basics of investing, including stocks, mutual funds, retirement plans, and college savings plans.

***Responsible Money* resource**	**CCSS in Mathematics**	**CEE® Standards**	**Jump$tart® Standards**	**C3 Framework for Social Studies**	**Family and Consumer Sciences National Standards**
Activity 6.2: Financial Terms		Financial Investing 1,2,3,4	Investing 1,2,4		Consumer & Family Resources 2.7.1
Activity 6.3: Understanding the Risks		Financial Investing 5,6,7,11	Risk Management and Insurance 1	Economics D2.Eco.2.6-8	Consumer & Family Resources 2.7.5
Activity 6.4: Dollar Cost Averaging	6.SP.B.5.C 6.NS.B.3 7.RP.A.2	Financial Investing 4	Investing 1,3	Economics D2.Eco.1.6-8	Consumer & Family Resources 2.5.4 2.7.6
Activity 6.5: How to Invest		Financial Investing 3,6,10,13	Investing 3,4	Economics D2.Eco.1.6-8 D2.Eco.9.9-12	Consumer & Family Resources 2.3.1 2.5.3
Activity 6.6: Investing for Retirement	8.F.B.5	Financial Investing 7,11	Investing 1,2	Economics D2.Eco.1.9-12 D2.Eco.2.6-8	Consumer & Family Resources 2.6.2 2.7.6
Activity 6.7: Saving for College		Financial Investing 7,11	Investing 1,2	Economics D2.Eco.1.9-12 D2.Eco.2.6-8	Consumer & Family Resources 2.7.2 2.7.6

PHOTO CREDITS

Pages 3, 9 and 14:
Thanks to Sharon McCutcheon @sharonmccutcheon for making this photo available freely on Unsplash.

Pages 15 and 26:
Thanks to Avinash Kumar @ashishjha for making this photo available freely on Unsplash.

Pages 27 and 39:
Thanks to Andre Taissin @andretaissin for making this photo available freely on Unsplash.

Pages 41 and 57:
Thanks to Campaign Creators @campaign_creators for making this photo available freely on Unsplash.

Pages 59 and 74:
Thanks to rupixen.com @rupixen for making this photo available freely on Unsplash.

Pages 75 and 93:
Thanks to Patrick Weissenberger @ricktap for making this photo available freely on Unsplash.

About the Author

Ron Wright earned a Bachelor of Science in electrical engineering from Purdue University in West Lafayette, Indiana. After working as an engineer and manufacturing facilitator for several years, he decided to pursue his interest in financial services. He began by obtaining his life & health insurance license and then his series 6, 63, and 65 licenses. He went on to serve as a financial advisor and licensed banker. After several years in the field, he then pursued a career in education. Wright obtained his Illinois state teaching license and a Master of Arts in education from Governors State University in 2011. Since then, he has been teaching elementary and middle school. A highly regarded teacher in his community, his students excel and achieve at a high level because of his strong belief in education, as well as his enthusiasm and passion for teaching. He enjoys spending time with his family, coaching baseball, and walking his dog, Twix, who is the company logo for Bear Wright LLC.

Made in United States
Cleveland, OH
06 November 2026

47771495R00073